Advance
FOR THE PEOPLE

"If we take this book seriously and ground our differing perspectives in its principles as we debate, our country will be the better for it. Chadwick's carefully considered suggestions can serve as a springboard for a more respectful and considered dialogue. He argues convincingly that the surest way to authoritarian rule is by defining the community in-group narrowly, and instead advocates for broad inclusiveness. This book proposes that effective leadership rests on foundations not only of inclusion, but also of empathy, authenticity, listening, inspiration, and empowerment. Chadwick's wide-ranging and thought-provoking assessment of today's most polarizing issues should be read by everyone interested in better understanding the actions required to preserve our democracy."

Sim Sitkin, Michael W. Krzyzewski Professor and Principal, Behavioral Science and Policy Center, Duke University

"This book is a must-read for everyone running for any type of office. Debates and arguments from people on either side of the aisle will be well-informed and productive after having read it."

Kumar Mehta, author and principal at Bridges Insight, and Senior Research Fellow, Center for the Digital Future, University of Southern California

"What Chadwick does well is set up the 'higher-order' goal of wanting a better America for everyone as the reason behind his thesis. As a result, any reasonable reader will follow his argument to the end. They may not like it, but won't be able to dismiss it either."

Will Leach, author and CEO of The Mindstate Group

"I have read this book twice. Simon Chadwick's thinking and his ability to weave together so many important strands into a coherent manifesto are truly brilliant."

Kathi Love, former CEO of GfK Mediamark Research and Intelligence

For *the* People

A Citizen's Manifesto to
Shaping Our Nation's Future

SIMON CHADWICK

RIVER GROVE
BOOKS

This publication is designed to provide accurate and authoritative information in regard to the subject matter covered. It is sold with the understanding that the publisher and author are not engaged in rendering legal, accounting, or other professional services. Nothing herein shall create an attorney-client relationship, and nothing herein shall constitute legal advice or a solicitation to offer legal advice. If legal advice or other expert assistance is required, the services of a competent professional should be sought.

Published by River Grove Books
Austin, TX
www.rivergrovebooks.com

Distributed by River Grove Books

Design and composition by Greenleaf Book Group and Rachael Brandenburg
Cover design by Greenleaf Book Group and Rachael Brandenburg
Cover image: ©iStock/erhui1979

Publisher's Cataloging-in-Publication data is available.

Print ISBN: 978-1-63299-269-7

eBook ISBN: 978-1-63299-270-3

First Edition

To my wife, Johnnie,
who is my rock,
my biggest fan,
and my biggest critic

Democratic: Relating to or supporting democracy or its principles

Demos: the people

Kratia: power, rule

> *"Government of the people, by the people, for the people."*
>
> —ABRAHAM LINCOLN

Libertarianism: Political philosophy that takes individual liberty to be the primary political value

Libertarians: Classical liberals who strongly emphasize the individual right to liberty

> —BRITANNICA

Libertas: freedom

Table of Contents

PART ONE

The Case for a Different Way

1

America in an Exceptional Crisis

America has always held itself up to be exceptional. And, in many ways, it is. America for two centuries has been a land of ingenuity, invention, and dynamism, a country where technology, industry, culture, and the arts have combined to produce a place unlike any other on this planet.

Politically, America has also been a beacon for the concept of democracy, albeit one that is wrapped in a very Roman construct of the "republic." Here the media is free and the people are protected by a constitution that, among other things, sanctifies freedom of speech, freedom of assembly, freedom of worship, and freedom from authoritarian overreach in the form of search. The very word "freedom" is baked into the central idea of "these United States," even if its practice right from the beginning was rather selective. It is a land where, theoretically, people are limited only by their own imaginations and where opportunity is rife. Its people are proud of this America, as they should be, and are proud to be called patriots.

But the reality is that America today is broken. Worse than that, it is exceptionalism gone haywire. The political system crafted by the Founding Fathers has mutated into a governmental structure overrun by special interests and their money, which, in its turn, acts like the poison of a very virulent insect and renders politicians incapable of acting in the best interests of both their constituents and the country as a whole. The system that was supposed to balance power between governmental institutions has become one of stasis—the inability of government to actually govern. The country is divided as never before into opposing camps succored by social media bubbles in which people only converse with and receive ideas from those similar in outlook to themselves. A Congress that, at the House level, has been so gerrymandered as to make the concept of representative government laughable is rendered incapable of dealing with the nation's most pressing issues. And the public, so fed up with politics as usual, has elected—via a very broken electoral college construct—a president who has shown himself to be a narcissistic incompetent who has single-handedly ceded America's leadership on the world stage to the Chinese and the Russians.

As wealth inequality has spiraled out of control—exacerbated by tax reform that blatantly favors the rich—and social mobility has dried up, poverty and racial inequality have persisted even as unemployment statistics have trended downward. Persistent, chronic problems that uniquely plague American society, such as mass shootings in schools or public arenas, remain unaddressed, even as the electorate demands reform. Americans are ten times more likely to be killed by guns than are citizens of other developed countries,[1] and yet this is supposed to be taken as normal, and demands for reform are met with hysterical responses from the National Rifle Association (NRA) and inaction by politicians who are in its pockets.

Other persistent, chronic problems are met with the same inability—or, worse, hostility—to deal with them. Consider, for instance, lack of access to health care due to exorbitant insurance rates or lack of insurance. When the Obama administration tried to deal with this issue (in a very American way),

---

1   Erin Grinshteyn and David Hemenway. "Violent Death Rates: The United States Compared to Other High-Income OECD Countries, 2010." *The American Journal of Medicine* 129, no. 3, 2016.

it was howled down as "socialism" and became the focus of innumerable Republican attempts to sink it. The fact that the USA spends three times as much on health care as other developed nations but with outcomes that woefully lag behind them?[2] Ignored. Or that we have a secondary education system that is completely broken and also has outcomes well below those of our competitors? Ignored. Or that our social safety net is under constant attack by those who need to finance tax breaks for the wealthy? Ignored. And now, how about an Environmental Protection Agency (EPA) where the man initially appointed by Trump to run it made no bones about his desire to destroy it, and a president who clearly has no patience for environmental stewardship?

Amidst all of this, great swaths of the population get left behind. After the Civil War, newly freed African-Americans possessed 0.5 percent of the wealth of the nation. Today, African-Americans own between 1 percent and 2 percent of the national wealth. In 2010, the median wealth of black families in the United States was $3,900, while that of their white counterparts was $97,000.[3] Yet there are also white families all across "flyover" America who themselves are suffering as automation and offshoring take away their manufacturing jobs and leave them living in shells that were formerly their towns and communities. In both black and white communities faced with infrastructural decay and poverty, crime persists and is fed by the opiate of drugs—whether they be cocaine, heroin, meth, or prescription opioids. This leads to an increasing effort on the part of law enforcement to maintain control and, in some places, the militarization of police. Very quickly, there is a lack of social discourse, a weakening of trust in social and governmental institutions, and increasingly virulent outbreaks of "other-ism."

"Other-ism," at its simplest, is the attribution of blame to others in society who appear different from you, for all the ills that you yourself suffer. Who these "others" are has varied over the course of American history. In

---

2   Center for Medicare and Medicare Services, 2018.

3   Economic Policy Institute, June 20, 2012.

the early days of the colonies, they were the indigenous Americans. In the Jim Crow era, they were African-Americans. Then there were the Italians, Greeks, Eastern Europeans, Chinese, Japanese, and the bogeymen of them all, the Jews. Today, it is Muslims, Middle Easterners, South Asians, and—yes—the Jews.

The issue with "other-ism" is not so much that it exists. Sad to say, there will always be those who wish to pin the blame for their ills, real or imagined, on those who are different than they are. There will always be those who will follow the leadership of some crackpot white supremacist or cult leader. No, the real issue with "other-ism" is when it is used by mainstream politicians either to gain power or to cover up their own incompetence or venality. When that happens, "other-ism" awakens deep-seated, vague prejudices that allow people to turn aside from societal norms, or even their own affirmed values, in a desperate attempt to make themselves heard. That in turn can lead to quiet acquiescence from other political leaders and, ultimately, the population at large. And when that happens, "other-ism" becomes very dangerous indeed.

For those with historical memory, we saw this in Germany and Italy in the 1930s, and we see it in the long-running conflicts in the Middle East and in tribal conflicts in Africa (think of the 1994 massacres in Rwanda, for example). We also see it in the rise of non-state actors such as ISIS, which is entirely based on "other-ism." And now it is right here on our own doorstep in America. From the outset, Donald Trump used "other-ism" to anchor his campaign, talking about criminal, rapist Mexicans and the expulsion of Muslims and, in so doing, calling out the demons in those feeling left behind. No wonder he had difficulty in fully condemning the white supremacists involved in the Unite the Right rally in Charlottesville, Virginia, since these were the very people fanning the flames of the fire he had started. That, and his blatant misogyny, would have been bad enough. But then a pivotal event happened: Evangelical Christians decided to turn a blind eye to all of this in order to further their own political agenda. Once they did this, they gave the perfect political cover to Republicans in Congress to do the same: hold their noses in the name of furthering their agenda. And so, acquiescence started to take hold. The rot set in, and America is at war with itself, in danger of jettisoning its institutions, political processes, and values and building an economic (and real) wall around itself as it abandons its world leadership position and blames everyone else for its woes.

The net—and very ironic—result of all this is that, in the midst of an economic boom, America is filled with anger and hate, families avoid politics at all costs at the Thanksgiving table, and political and social discourse has ground to a halt. Worse, the United States of America is now rated as a "flawed democracy,"[4] and the think tank Freedom House talks of democracy worldwide facing its "most serious crisis in decades" as a result.

In a nutshell, America has become a country lacking in both physical and psychological security, and the world has become more insecure as a result. *And insecurity is a clear and present danger to world peace and stability.*

---

4   The Economist Intelligence Unit Democracy Index 2018.

2

Insecurity and Maslow's Hierarchy

In 1943, the American psychologist Abraham Maslow published a paper called "A Theory of Human Motivation" that would go on to shape much of the way in which scientists and sociologists would view basic human decision making. The concept at the center of the paper was *Maslow's hierarchy of needs*, which was essentially a pyramid describing human needs from the most basic (physiological—such as shelter and food) to the most elevated (the need for self-esteem and the ability to "actualize" one's self to greater achievement).

At the core of the hierarchy is the concept of "security," whether that be physical, social, or psychological. It is this author's belief that this concept lies at the very heart of human existence at both individual and societal levels. An individual cannot experience security if the society he or she lives in is not secure (just ask a modern Syrian). And a society cannot be secure unless its members are secure (ask any Venezuelan).

If we are to find a way out of our current, potentially existential, crisis, therefore, we really do need to understand the concept of security and how it applies to society and government. And we need to understand what *real* security looks like as opposed to that which is secured at the point of a gun.

Let's take a look at what Maslow has to say on this subject from the individual's point of view—best summed up in his pyramid.

SELF-
ACTUALIZATION
morality, creativity,
spontaneity, acceptance,
experience purpose, meaning,
and inner potential

SELF-ESTEEM
confidence, achievement, respect for
others, the need to be a unique indiviual

LOVE AND BELONGING
friendship, family, intimacy, sense of connection

SAFETY AND SECURITY
health, employment, property, family, and social ability

PHYSIOLOGICAL NEEDS
breathing, food, water, shelter, clothing, sleep

Maslow's Hierarchy of Needs

The most basic of our needs are **Physiological**, things that most of us in the West take for granted, such as a roof over our heads, food on our table, clean drinking water, clothes on our backs, and air that we can breathe. In many parts of the world, even these needs are not adequately met, meaning that the baseline of societal security is absent.

For most of us in the United States, however, these needs are met. But there are two "buts." But no. 1 is that there are still thousands of people living on the streets of the richest nation in the world who do not have a roof over their heads, access to regular food, or even clothes on their backs. Talk to the woman huddled in a doorway in the middle of a nor'easter snowstorm in New York who, unless she is rescued by police, will surely die of hypothermia; or to the residents of a tent city in the woods a few hundred yards from a shopping mall in Durham, North Carolina. Witness the armies of homeless in prosperous cities such as San Francisco or Portland, Oregon, many of whom have been "transported" there by towns and cities in the Midwest through the simple mechanism of giving them a one-way bus ticket and telling them not to return.[5] A society that tolerates this "even for the least among us" (to paraphrase Matthew 25:40) cannot be held to be secure.

But no. 2 is that, alone among prosperous Western societies, the United States does not provide an adequate barrier against its citizens slipping through the net and finding themselves without these basic needs. Only in the United States can you suffer from a serious illness and find yourself bankrupt and homeless as a result. This—and other roads to security perdition, such as the loss of a job—means that many Americans live in the shadow of fear that they, too, might join those on the streets of San Francisco or in the woods of Durham. And fear does not translate to security.

The second level up in the pyramid is that of **Safety and Security**, and it is arguably here that governments have (or should have) the most interaction with their citizens. This is the bedrock that allows for individuals to feel that they can grow in a secure environment and, as a consequence, so can society and the economy. Safety and security can be summarized as the absence of fear combined with the freedom to grow. It does not just relate to physical security (although that is paramount) but also encompasses the security afforded by good health, good education, good job prospects, and

---

5   Sadly, Western destination cities such as San Francisco now indulge in this practice too. *The Guardian*, December 20, 2017.

overall financial well-being. If we have all of these, we are equipped not only to take advantage of opportunities but also to "weather the slings and arrows of outrageous fortune," as Shakespeare would have it.

As we will examine in more detail later on, here too the United States falls far behind other advanced societies and lets its citizens down. While the country is the most robustly armed in the world and so provides confidence in its ability to fend off external threats, internally its violent crime rate exceeds those of its peers by massive margins, its health outcomes are worse, it lags educationally, and the inequality of wealth between one tiny fraction of the population and the masses remains frightening in the extreme. Few are expecting the French Revolution here any time soon, but remember that it was propelled by economic hardship and gross inequality of wealth. "Let them eat cake" might just as well be the mantra of the ruling classes in America today.

On these two fundamental foundations—physiological needs and safety and security—rests the entire ability of both individuals and society to achieve the upper echelons of the pyramid: **Love and Belonging**, **Self-Esteem**, and **Self-Actualization**. It is very difficult to feel that you are loved or that you belong if you live in fear of losing your security, and near impossible to achieve that esteem that then enables you to translate all that you are into someone who leaves a legacy of meaningful contribution to the world.

If you are homeless and without education or income, you are unlikely to become an astrophysicist. If you are African-American and live in the projects, your access to a high-quality education is more limited, and your likelihood to secure financial independence is reduced. If you are sick and cannot get decent health care, your entire existence revolves around avoiding the dark pit of homelessness while remaining alive—not much room there for self-actualization.

We will examine these three upper levels in the context of what government should and should not do for its citizens later in the book. The key takeaway here is that "government of the people, by the people, for the people" needs, if it is to be successful, to take all the levels of Maslow's hierarchy into consideration as it endeavors to create the conditions for society's well-being.

But what if government's aim is not the well-being of all its people? What if it is not of, by, and for the people? What if it is for the few who actually govern? Then a totally new set of rules takes precedence.

3

How to Become a Dictator

I n 2011, the political scientists Bruce Bueno de Mesquita and Alastair Smith published one of the most seminal books about politics, called *The Dictator's Handbook: Why Bad Behavior Is Almost Always Good Politics.* The book built on a theory posited by the authors and fellow academics Randolph Siverson and James Morrow called the *selectorate theory.* Together, these tracts could almost be republished as *The Idiot's Guide to Why Trump Won.*

Selectorate theory states that politicians gain and retain power based on the size and actions of three groups of people—the *nominal selectorate,* the *real selectorate,* and the *winning coalition.*

These may be described as follows:

GROUP	ALSO KNOWN AS	US EXAMPLE
Nominal selectorate	Interchangeables	Total electorate
Real selectorate	Influentials	Those who vote
Winning coalition	Essentials	Financiers Voters in critical states

In a democracy such as the United States, the nominal selectorate (also known as interchangeables) is the total number of people who can vote. The power they hold is in the fact that they have a vote, but the real questions are (1) whether they *will* vote; (2) whether they *can* vote; and (3) whether their vote will *count*. Whether they *will* vote is obviously a factor of how much a candidate can motivate them to do so, as well as the degree to which the candidate can reach them through advertising and an on-the-ground campaign, both of which are dependent on money. Whether they *can* vote today is dependent on local and state laws on early voting, availability of voting stations, and purging of voter rolls—all of which are things that state legislatures delight in fiddling with to maximize their own party advantage. Whether their vote *counts* depends on the drawing of voting districts, again something that state legislatures monkey with on an ongoing basis. For example, a recent court ruling found that North Carolina's legislature had drawn that state's voting districts with "surgical precision" to mute the effectiveness of the African-American and Democratic vote, resulting in a supermajority of Republicans despite their benefiting from a voting advantage of only 52–48 percent statewide.

Obviously, the nominal selectorate is only as powerful as the degree to which it gets off the couch and actually goes to the polls. Those that do so are the *real selectorate* or "influentials." These are the people that politicians and their moneyed supporters need to win over. But, even then, they are not created equal (at least not in the American electoral system). Some districts and states are much more important than others to tilt one way or another—they are the ones that will sway the result in the electoral college. Sometimes, as in 2016, the popular vote will swing one way and the electoral college will vote the other. In this instance, you could say that there was the real selectorate and the *real, real selectorate*—that is, those 70,000 voters in key states that swung the election Donald Trump's way. In some ways, Hillary Clinton's downfall was that she miscalculated which states really constituted the real selectorate.

There was another real selectorate at play in the 2016 election as well—one that Trump played brilliantly. This was the disaffected white working-class vote in flyover states that had lost their economic security. Conjuring "the others" (Mexicans, Muslims, the Chinese) and promising magical solutions (the wall, rejuvenation of coal and steel, and mass deportations), Trump awoke a part of the nominal selectorate that had hitherto been ignored and brought it into his real selectorate. Clinton missed that one completely, even going so far as to call them "deplorables"—probably a fatal mistake.

But what Trump did in 2016 was even more powerful: Not only did he awaken a portion of the electorate that had remained quasi-dormant for years, but he brought them into his *winning coalition* (also known as the "essentials"). This is the bringing together of disparate groups around a narrative, or a story, that, however briefly, binds them behind the candidate and propels them to vote for him or her, *even if much of what that candidate stands for goes against their core beliefs.*

In an excellent article published in *The Guardian*, George Monbiot puts forward a theory that societies are driven by narratives.[6] Inevitably, they are stories of restoration that go like this: Everything's a mess; here's who is responsible; here's how to fix it; here's who will fix it (the hero or heroes); the hero(es) will fight the bad guys and win; and everybody will have a much more prosperous future. The "here's how to fix it" part is usually based on a Utopian theory—restore the monarchy, trust in a strong man, trust in collectivism or socialism—and the heroes are either individuals or the people as a whole.

The point here is that the story has to hang together. It has to be cohesive, starting with making the targeted selectorate believe that everything is a mess and then taking them through to a solution and a hero who is going to miraculously make everything better. Once people get the narrative into their minds and really start to buy into it, presentation of contrary facts becomes

---

6   "How Do We Get Out of This Mess?" *The Guardian*, September 11, 2017.

not only inconvenient but downright dangerous and must be expunged. We believe that deriding such "inconvenient truths" (to borrow a phrase from Al Gore) as "fake news" is a modern phenomenon, but in actuality it has been going on for as long as politics has been around, whether representative or not. And presentation of "alternative facts" is also a long-established tradition, the main differences being that, today, these circulate with the speed of light via the wonder of social media, and barefaced lying in public has become the new and tolerated norm.

Trump's narrative was classic. America was in a terrible state (or "carnage," as he put it in his inauguration speech), "others" were responsible (Mexicans, all immigrants, China, Europe), only he could fix it, and then America would be "great again." The story resonated big-time with the "deplorables," but Trump still had to build a winning coalition out of the selectorate. He was facing sixteen other candidates for the presidential nomination and was winning despite most Republicans voting for one of his rivals. Put another way, the "deplorables" were carrying him, but he needed another, highly compelling, story to bring in another key part of the winning coalition.

If we study forms of government going back centuries, it is clear that they fall on a linear spectrum. At one end are pure democracies (which, though rare, do exist) and, at the other, outright dictatorship. In between, there are a myriad of other options, including "flawed democracies," oligarchies, and absolute monarchies.

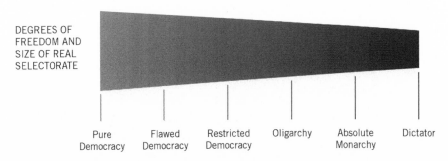

The Real Selectorate in Differing Forms of Government

Pure or "full" democracies, as defined by the Economist Intelligence Unit (EIU) in its annual democracy rankings, not only offer the greatest degrees of freedom to their population but also have the largest real selectorates, ensuring as far as possible that each vote counts as much as the next. Examples of such societies include most Scandinavian countries, as well as Canada, Australia, and New Zealand. Flawed democracies, of which the United States is one according to the EIU, tend to limit freedoms more (for example, the ability to vote) and work to reduce the size of the real selectorate in favor of the party in power. If we take this to the other extreme of the spectrum—dictatorship or even absolute monarchy, as in Saudi Arabia—the size of the real selectorate is highly reduced, and basic freedoms are severely constrained. In many such countries, the facade of democracy is maintained to provide a loincloth for the regime but counts for nothing in terms of the reality of government or everyday life. Russia and Venezuela would be good examples in our modern world.

As the EIU points out, the status of democracy in the world is not static. Indeed, after growing for many years, it is now on the retreat in many parts of the world. The point to be made here, however, is that democracy *cannot retreat on its own*. Nor can it necessarily retreat because of the actions of one man or one group, unless it is overthrown in a violent coup. Usually, the group concerned—or the wannabe dictator—*uses democracy* to infiltrate the system and then works to change it from within, most often by challenging and dismantling the institutions designed to protect the democratic system. These would include a functioning and independent judiciary as well as a free press. Adolf Hitler did this in the 1930s in Germany, as did Hugo Chávez in Venezuela in 1999. It could be argued the Nationalist Party in South Africa did the same in 1948—even though they maintained a democratic system, it was a restricted democracy where only whites could vote, leading to a dictatorship of the many by the few. In all of these, the unique principle of democracy—that the minority should be protected from and by the majority—was thrown out the window.

The most important thing to realize here, however, is that none of these players could have gotten away with what they were doing (moving their countries inexorably from democracy to some more limited form of political freedom) *were it not for the complicit acceptance of those in the establishment, in politics, in business, in religion, and in the population as a whole.* Had the churches not remained quiet in the face of increasing harassment of the Jews in Germany, maybe the middle classes would have realized that what was happening was unacceptable—and maybe they would have given spines to their political representatives. Had English-speaking South Africans spoken up in protest at the draconian laws of apartheid, maybe they would have awoken the conscience of the broader white population.

Trump recognized and depended upon this in his own campaign. The "deplorables" alone would not have taken him across the line, either in the popular vote or the electoral college. What Trump needed was for the Republican establishment to swallow their distaste, hold their noses, and endorse him. This included not only critical members of Congress (Paul Ryan, Mitch McConnell, and Marco Rubio, for example) but also the business establishment and—very important—Evangelicals. Once the Christian right was persuaded to put aside moral objections in favor of getting the right-wing agenda enacted, Trump now had a real chance of winning the election.

The problem with such a strategy is what comes next.

The primary goal of any leader, any politician, is "once in power, stay in power." To do that, they must show that they are providing results for the winning coalition. In the crudest circumstances—say, in a dictatorship where the dictator was brought to power by a small cadre of army officers—this means enriching those who brought him (or, more rarely, her) into power. Robert Mugabe, erstwhile ruler of Zimbabwe, did this by "redistributing" white-owned farmland to his fighters and his cabinet ministers. Various Latin American dictators enriched their military elites. At the other end of the scale, pure democracy ruling parties have very large winning coalitions (i.e., all the people who voted for them) and so must deliver on the promises that got them elected in the first place. This usually means that they provide the "public" goods demanded by their electorates, such as welfare benefits, universal health care, or universal education. The dictator, on the other hand, will usually convert these "public goods" (that is, the tax revenues of the country) into "private goods" to enrich his cronies or, in more polite language, his small winning coalition.

But what about the flawed democracy? How does the politician in power pay off his or her winning coalition? In this instance, the answer is more nuanced and usually involves a mix of real "payments" to those that really count and "smoke and mirrors" to those that only count at election time.

Let us take Mr. Trump as our example. His winning coalition was the "deplorables" backed up by the silent acquiescence of the Republican establishment, inclusive of Evangelicals and the money men bankrolling Republican campaigns. In order to keep all of these behind him, he needed to combine "real" payments to the Republicans, Evangelicals, and money brokers and "smoke and mirror" payments to the base. The former involved tax cuts (a religious tenet of being a Republican but also of direct benefit to the money brokers) and the appointment of a conservative judge to the Supreme Court. But what to offer to the base? It was unlikely that he could really reopen factories in rust belt communities or bring about a resurgence of coal in West Virginia. But what he *could* do was to make symbolic moves using all the shibboleths that so enrage his base—trade pacts, immigration, and nasty foreign countries. And so you have the withdrawal from the Trans-Pacific Partnership (TPP) trade agreement, the renegotiation of NAFTA, the much-touted wall, deportations, and tariffs. Viewed from a non-Trumpian angle, all of these could be said to be deleterious to American interests in the long run, but in the short run they act to pay off the base and keep them solidly in his column.

Payment of the winning coalition, therefore, is one element of staying in power. But invariably there are other things that need doing, such as weakening the remaining institutions that could thwart your agenda or, even worse, turn you out of power. In most erstwhile democracies, there are three such institutions that need to be dealt with: parliament, the judiciary, and the press. In Vladimir Putin's Russia, all three are now subservient to the presidency. In Venezuela, a fixed referendum deprived the legitimate parliament of its powers. In China, all three institutions sit squarely underneath the Communist Party apparatus, which now is also dominated by the presidency.

In the present-day United States, the Trump administration is at war with two of these branches of government and society (the judiciary and the press), while the Republican-controlled Senate has already thrown in the towel. In silently acquiescing to Trump's agenda in order to further their own, following the 2016 election, the Republicans in Congress allowed their president to redefine the party itself. Only a Democratic swing in the 2018 midterm elections started to turn the clock back, although to what effect remains to be seen. In the meantime, Trump is at war with his own intelligence community and continues to wage war against the media while at the same time using those elements that favor him—Fox News and his own Twitter account—to great effect. All of this is classic strategy. Make no mistake, President Trump is no idiot. He plays the *Dictator's Handbook* game to perfection.

But how could Trump even get into a position to play this game, given all the protections of the Constitution designed to prevent such dominance? And given that there is a huge other political party out there that commands more than 50 percent of the popular vote? Yes, there is the role of money. Yes, there is the politicization of the judiciary. Yes, there is blatant gerrymandering. And yes, there is a huge media machine run out of Australia that acts as his PR agency (aka Fox News). Even so, it was not inevitable that this should happen.

The one missing component in our narrative is the negligent abandonment by the Democratic Party of both its core constituencies, and its misunderstanding of the key needs of critical sectors of the population.

4

Democratic Abdication of Power

On the surface, Democrats have no excuse for being locked out of power, not only in Washington but also in governors' mansions and legislatures around the country. After all, they have the largest nominal selectorate in the United States, even in Texas, which has been a red state for decades. But in state after state, they have a smaller real selectorate and an even smaller winning coalition. Why?

There are many good reasons that can be offered but which really don't get to the nub of the problem. One that would resonate in many states is blatant gerrymandering. In states such as Texas and North Carolina, it is true that ruling Republican legislatures drew electoral districts that threw both states into permanent "red" status despite their populations showing a much different disposition. But, if that is true, how did the Democrats lose these state legislatures in the first place?

You will remember that the nominal selectorate (i.e., the total electorate in the United States) is also known as the "interchangeables." And that's exactly how the Democrats treated them—as interchangeable. A party that has its base in the major conurbations—New York, Los Angeles, San

Francisco, and Chicago—ignored not only the flyover white populations but also their own base. Blacks and Hispanics naturally gravitate to the Democrats but, in turn, are almost uniformly taken for granted by the party to whom they pledge allegiance. The era of Obama saw this constituency turn out in droves, but post-Obama, the party paid little attention to their needs, instead counting on their vote as a right. The black vote did not switch to Trump—instead, they just did not turn out in the numbers that were there in 2008 and 2012.

Similarly, the Clinton campaign singularly failed to convert the young "interchangeables" into voting "influentials." All the enthusiasm that had built up around Bernie Sanders in this particular demographic was squandered, despite a late swing by Clinton to positions more in line with Sanders's own thinking. Once again, they did not turn out in the numbers expected.

Worse than ignoring or, at the very least, taking for granted these vital core constituencies, the Clinton campaign made two other crucial mistakes. The first of these was to be tone deaf to what was important to these two groups. Viewed in Maslovian terms, the campaign doubled down on issues that represented "safety" (which, as you will recall, is the second rung up the pyramid from physiological well-being) and ignored these groups' needs for belonging and esteem. So they talked about preserving Obamacare, extending welfare, and strengthening education—that is, when they were not slamming Trump for being a boorish, bullying misogynist. What they emphatically did *not* do was to embrace either the black community or young whites and give them a feeling of belonging in the Democratic fold. Precious little was said about racism or police-on-black violence or the fact that blacks still owned a tiny proportion of the national wealth. Until too late, issues really important to the young, such as universal health care, were scrupulously avoided. Having beaten Sanders, Clinton carried straight on as if he had not existed. Failing to show respect for these two groups—failing to make them feel as if they really belonged in the House of Democrats— cost Clinton badly at the polls, as people simply failed to turn up and vote.

Maybe that would not have mattered so much were it not for the second mistake Clinton made. To be fair to her, it was a mistake that the Democrats had been making for years, but this time it really bit them in the rear. *They ignored Trump's new base.* Even worse, Clinton herself insulted it. Poor whites in flyover, rust belt states have not been a Democrat priority since LBJ was president. At no time was there any attempt to make this group feel that their priorities, their lives, mattered. Not only were they not given esteem or respect, but the Democratic campaign did not really address issues of safety with them. To be fair, Bernie Sanders did make inroads among this group and probably could have won at least enough of them over to prevent the electoral college debacle that followed. But once he was consigned to the sidelines, there was precious little attention paid, to the extent that Clinton's campaign ignored some of these states completely.

This error left the way completely open to Trump to fill the gap. And what did he fill it with? "Other-ism." "Your problems are the fault of others (foreign countries, Muslims, Mexicans); only I can fix it." "Nobody's laughing at us now." And indeed, now we are not.

Clinton's deafness, her taking the black and young vote for granted, and her dissing of the base that Trump was so assiduously courting led not only to an attrition of her winning coalition but also to a fatal complacency in which Democrats talked to themselves and were outplayed locally, at the state level, and nationally. When Republicans accuse Democrats and "liberals" of being elitist, they are not only deploying coded language that enrages the disenfranchised base. They are, unfortunately, describing a reality in the Democratic Party that needs fixing, and soon.

The question is: how?

In losing the 2016 election, as well as legislatures and governors' mansions all around the country, the Democrats have given over the nation to a political and cultural desert in which the rules are played by *The Dictator's Handbook* and where Maslow's hierarchy applies only to the wealthy. Key institutions are under attack—not least the judiciary and the press—as the country slips ever further from what Lincoln described as a "perfect union." Never before has the country been so viscerally divided to the point where politics is now a banned subject at most Thanksgiving dinner tables. And never before have those divisions been so inflamed and enhanced by the speed of social media and the degree to which it separates people into their own little bubbles. Barring the emergence of a real third party, it will be down to the Democrats to work out a strategy through which to reverse what is, in part, a mess of their own making.

Come the 2018 midterms, it seemed the Democrats had indeed worked out such a strategy. Sweeping the House with a wave of progressive female candidates, hope was born that a real power to rein in Trump and the Republicans had been put in place. As the rejuvenated Democrats in Congress initiate legislation and inquiries designed to undo Trumpism, there is excitement abroad that the United States may have dodged the bullet of authoritarian dictatorship. The Constitution has indeed worked. However, this does not necessarily mean that the damage done will be easily reversed. The system that led to this state of events, and the flaws in that system, will not be changed overnight. Money will still make its presence in the electoral system felt; gerrymandering will still exist unless Congress shows some unprecedented backbone and changes the rules; media oligarchs will still try to bend a credulous electorate to their will; and politicians will still play on group insecurities to get themselves into power while having no intention whatsoever of actually dealing with those insecurities. Attention to Maslow's hierarchy will continue to be partial, with Republicans considering the needs of their wealthy backers and Democrats ignoring white flyovers. The rules of *The Dictator's Handbook* will still be the primary playbook.

This brings us to our central thesis: In order to break out of this spiral in which our democracy becomes ever more flawed, we need to adopt a new system (or, indeed, philosophy) of politics, one that aspires to pure democracy, expands the winning coalition to its widest point, and acts upon

Maslow's hierarchy to the benefit of the whole population, not just favored groups. If the Democrats want to regain serious relevance, they would do well to adopt and boldly enact this new system and philosophy.

But, in order to reach this more perfect union, there is one more element of American life that we have to take into account—the dream of liberty.

5

The Liberty in Libertarianism

M ost political discussion around the world revolves around a distinction between Left and Right. How this is understood is often the product of circumstances and political history in each country. For example, what is seen as left-wing in American politics would be seen in much of Europe as mild right-wing. What the British see as left-wing would be discounted in the United States as downright socialism (without any idea of what that word actually means). And what the British see as right-wing would be viewed in other countries as Christian Democracy or, in the US, as milquetoast centrism. Nonetheless, this is the main linguistic currency by which we describe politics around the world.

For our purposes, let us define the Left-Right axis this way. The Left tends to favor labor and the working person and is concerned about protecting the disadvantaged in life through the redistribution of wealth via the tax system and active government programs (social welfare, public health care, and free education). At its extreme, it can become "socialism," a system which—through government control of resources, the means of production, and the distribution of wealth—seeks to ensure the principle of "from each according to his means to each according to his needs." We will delve into the real meaning of socialism later on in the book. By contrast, the Right tends to favor capital, encouraging investment of capital into the economy through lower taxation of investors. It tends to prefer private solutions to key issues in society—for example, providing health care and infrastructure. At its extreme, it can drift toward "fascism," a system by which individual liberties are curtailed in favor of the functioning of the state, if necessary by force. There is an argument that the Left-Right spectrum is in fact not linear but circular, since the behaviors of the extreme Left and the extreme Right can be remarkably similar to one another. But this is a debate we will leave for others to have.

There is another axis, however, by which politics could and should be measured, and that is the distinction between authoritarianism and libertarianism. Authoritarians believe in the power of central government and in the rule of laws and regulations. They rely on law enforcement to ensure that society functions in the way they want it to and often rule by diktat. No aspect of society is out of bounds for the regulations they wish to impose. At the extreme, authoritarians can tilt toward totalitarianism (whether Left or Right), expunging democracy and civil liberties. Libertarians, on the other hand, believe that government should stay out of their lives as much as possible, only being there to meet key needs, while people are free to believe what they want, worship who they want, and just get on with their lives. They advocate "small government," preferring that key issues be resolved either at the community or market level. Taken to the extreme (which rarely exists for reasons we will see a little later), this can lead to anarchy.

If we overlay these two axes on one another, we suddenly see politics in an entirely different light. It's a bit like looking at a map and realizing that most people live in one area while wishing they lived in another.

The Four Types of Modern Government

Authoritarian

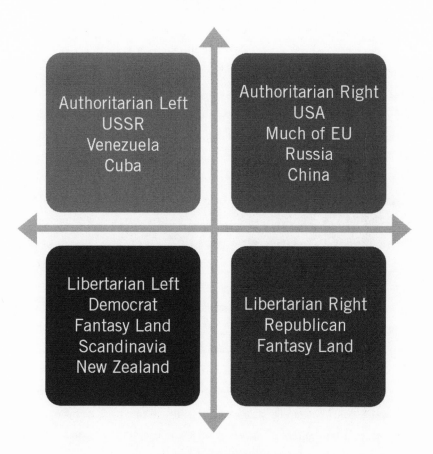

Libertarian

What may surprise most readers who believe, however loosely, in "democracy" is that the majority of the world lives under Authoritarian Right governments and societies. Most of these are societies in which conservative values rule but where government is primarily responsible for lawmaking, regulations, and rule-making. These are top-down types of societies, where government is expected to govern, the rule of law is paramount, and individual liberty is tolerated up to certain limits where it does not interfere with the smooth functioning of society. There is, however, a broad spectrum of Authoritarian Right societies, from Obama's America—where rule-making was designed to rein in practices, companies, and groups deemed to be destructive to society—to Trump's America, where regulations are relaxed on those same players but reinforced to regulate individual rights, such as that to abortion. Russia under Putin similarly lives under an Authoritarian Right regime, where central government is all-powerful and individual rights are curtailed. China under Xi is in the same position. But, interestingly, most EU countries, including the UK, also live under milder versions of the same idea—government exists to regulate in many different areas—even in France, down to how many hours a week you may work.

Authoritarian Right societies tend to function relatively well, but not always to the benefit of all sections of society. These are societies where *The Dictator's Handbook* is well understood by the governing elites, sometimes subtly and sometimes more brutally. Generally speaking, however, the winning coalition is restricted and the payoffs for those in it substantial. Those outside the coalition, such as the working poor, tend to get more of a raw deal.

Not all Authoritarian Right countries succeed. Those that take it to the extreme very often slide into a form of totalitarianism that subsumes and then snuffs out the candle of democracy and, along with it, the rights of minorities and dissenters. Examples today would include Egypt, Saudi Arabia, Turkey, and Iran. Hungary is not far behind.

However, the majority of Authoritarian Right nations are still democracies, ruling with a somewhat lighter touch. Take Britain, for example. Many Americans might express surprise that a country such as the UK would be classified as Authoritarian Right. After all, is this not the country of the National Health Service, a "socialist" manifestation of universal health care? Yes, it is. But it is also a country of considerable regulation, where the ruling elite have, for the most part, come from a very small sliver of society—primarily those educated at Eton and Oxford. (There is a standing joke in Britain that the only reason Oxford was connected by a freeway to London before Cambridge was because Oxford supplied the vast majority of its prime ministers.) The UK may be Authoritarian Right with a human face, but it is still most definitely Authoritarian Right.

If the top right-hand quadrant of our map is somewhat overpopulated, the top left-hand corner is the equivalent of a rust belt of political history. These are the societies and countries in which an Authoritarian Left has been tried and found severely wanting. They include the Soviet Union and its erstwhile empire as well as Cuba, Venezuela, Zimbabwe, and numerous other failed communist/socialist states. The funny thing here is that today, especially in the United States, we take this failure for granted, and the word "socialism" has become synonymous with "failed state." Yet, on a rereading of Engels and Marx, there was no initial intrinsic reason why these states should have failed. Indeed, at the time at which they were writing, imperialist capitalism (written here with no irony or political agenda) had been a great success for the few but was a source of misery for the many. Urban Britain at the time was incredibly wealthy, but its inhabitants lived in appalling slum conditions, with little in the way of health care or a social safety net. You got sick and either you died or you didn't—it was as simple as that. Life in that country's colonies was not much better, with staples being produced for consumption in the Western world by people living in abject poverty. Even in the United States, while fortunes were being made by the few, the majority were either living in slums or were under the yoke of slavery and, later, the laws of the Jim Crow era. From where Engels and Marx stood, a society built on the mantra "from each according to his ability to each according to his needs" did not seem crazy at all. So, why did most of the countries adopting the Marxist system fail so miserably?

There have been many learned books written about this conundrum, and I am by no means expert enough to produce the definitive answer. But one thing that does stand out is that, in order to ensure a fair distribution of wealth in any one society, it became clear there needed to be regulation—otherwise base human nature would take over. Once that became a necessity, huge bureaucracies arose around the idea of "planning," which invariably failed to meet their designated goals. Stalin's ideas of communal farming, for example, took no account of the need for efficiencies or of basics such as the weather. The worse the plans performed, the more the people needed to be "herded" into where the next plan said they needed to be—in the factories or on the farms or in the military or wherever the government, in its infinite wisdom, deemed was the most productive.

Try this in a democratic society and you will soon be voted out of power. Therefore, democracy had to be suppressed, and the selectorates and winning coalitions in communist countries became much, much smaller. Once that occurred, staying in power meant paying off a much smaller elite with much more power and riches. However, one of the side effects of restricting political life in this way is that freedom of thought and expression need to be suppressed. You can't have people out there exclaiming that the emperor has no clothes! Often, this brings on a purging of the so-called elites—academics, doctors, lawyers, clergy, and the like. As Karl Popper pointed out, this leads to ossification of technology, innovation, and, eventually, society and the economy.[7] Ultimately, the economies and political systems of these nations could not sustain autocratic rule by a corrupt and incompetent minority—a fact brilliantly leveraged by Ronald Reagan as he piled on the arms-race pressure on the Soviet Union. History tells us, therefore, that Authoritarian Left rarely works.

But what of the other two quadrants? These are truly fascinating, one for what it is promised to be but is not, and the other for how it actually works but with nobody believing it.

The bottom right-hand quadrant is, in the United States at least, political

---

7   Karl Popper. *The Open Society and Its Enemies* (London: Routledge, 1945).

Oz. This is the land in which conservative values rule—personal independence, faith in God, rule of law—but where the government gets the hell out of the way. Regulations and rules are frowned upon and are supposed to conform to the absolute minimum that will uphold basic law. This is the land that most conservative politicians invite their constituents to visit, and yet, post–election day, it is almost never there. Republicans are too wedded to the world of the Authoritarian Right to be able to deliver a Libertarian Right society, even if they wanted to. Some might argue that the rise of the Tea Party within the Republican ranks disproves this—that, indeed, there are politicians who thoroughly believe in this form of society and who, given enough time and support, would be able to deliver this type of government structure. Rand Paul would be an outstanding example of such a politician. Yet, the fact is, despite huge amounts of money backing Tea Party candidates, they have never amounted to more than an annoying (to establishment Republicans) clique in the House and, despite derailing some traditional Republican initiatives and ousting some establishment figures such as John Boehner, have not managed to wrest control of either the GOP or the government. Where they have managed to gain power, at state or local levels, the need to continue to listen to the wider selectorate often means they have to back off some of their more radical proposals.

A great example of this occurred in my home state of North Carolina not too long ago. Radical Republicans, having won supermajorities in the legislature and cowed the moderate GOP governor, Pat McCrory, into obedient submission, reacted to a City of Charlotte ordinance that, among other things, allowed transgender people to use public bathrooms according to their gender identification, not the gender of their birth. Horrified, the North Carolina House passed the now notorious HB2 bill that not only reversed this policy on a statewide basis but also restricted the ability of local governments to pass such ordinances in the first place. The backlash was enormous (ultimately costing McCrory the governor's mansion) but not only from LBGTQ communities, civil rights activists, and the Democratic Party—businesses also expressed their strong disapproval in a way that got everyone's attention: withholding revenue from the state by withdrawing planned developments, canceling cultural and sporting events, and refusing to do business with the state. The selectorate in this case was much wider than the legislature had imagined, and ultimately lawmakers were forced to repeal the measure.

What's interesting here is that avowed libertarian right-wingers would be so quick to both legislate on a matter that, philosophically at least, one would not think to be the purview of government to their way of thinking, and *then use state government to shut down local government's authority.* People who preach less government often fall into these two traps:

1. "Less government" usually means fewer regulations where business is concerned. But where social issues, especially regarding sex, are under the microscope, right-wing libertarians quickly revert to authoritianism. Access to abortion is perhaps the biggest litmus test of all here. It's almost as if the mantra is "We will not interfere with you in the boardroom, but in the bedroom, watch out!"

2. As soon as right-wing principles are challenged (especially when those principles are based on moral codes such as Evangelical Christian doctrine), right-wing libertarians will often use the power of government to assert centralized control to nullify the threat.

In truth, many of those who declare themselves to be right-wing libertarians are Authoritarian Right in a libertarian cloak.

Some may argue at this point that, on the contrary, in the face of despair at the way in which government has worked in this country for the last few decades (or has not), the electorate rebelled and elected the most right-wing libertarian government that we have seen in decades. After all, isn't that what Trump is doing? Viscerally cutting regulations, exiting constraining trade deals, and gutting the bureaucracy of central government? Yes, it is. But it is still boardroom vs. bedroom stuff. Trump and the Republican majority in Congress have provided a massive payback to the selectorate that really matters to them (moneyed business) through tax cuts and deregulation but has severely rolled back noncommercial degrees of freedom in areas such as abortion, the environment, and civil rights. Not only that, but the attack on societal institutions (the judiciary and the press especially), when put together with exactly where government is being gutted (Department of Energy) or attacked (Department of Justice), means that this is really a massive attempt to swing to totalitarianism under the guise of libertarianism. What is actually happening is the diametric opposite of what is being sold to the public.

So, if most nations, whether capitalist or socialist, are sitting squarely in the upper right-hand quadrant (Authoritarian Right), Authoritarian Left has been proven to be a bust, and Libertarian Right appears to be the equivalent of Oz, where does that leave our orphan bottom-left quadrant, Libertarian Left?

Many on the Right would argue, and with some justification, that this is just as much of a chimera as I claim the bottom-right to be. After all, they would argue, Bernie Sanders laid out a Libertarian Left agenda in the 2016 elections (as have numerous "progressive" Democrats before him), and it has always been found to be wanting. It all sounds so wonderful—universal health care, better schooling, free tuition, and broader social services—but who is going to pay for it? Given the alleged aversion to taxation in the United States, there is no way a government could deliver on all of this. In a phrase, it is "fiscally irresponsible."

Worse, it is "socialist." The ability of the right wing in this country to use this word as a slur—a meme with all sorts of dreadful connotations—is remarkable. Even more remarkable is their ability to paint other decidedly nonsocialist countries as being "socialist" and then to ascribe all sorts of problems to this supposedly deadly condition. Hence the UK health service (the NHS)—a universal, single-payer system that has been in place since the 1940s—is "socialist" and offers terrible service. Never mind that the UK has had numerous right-wing governments that would never dream of giving it up. Or that the NHS actually provides better overall health outcomes, using 7 percent of the GDP, than the US system does using 21 percent of national output. The German and French public pension deficits are painted as being the result of rampant "socialism," whereas they are in fact the result of demographic change and no different at all to the situation facing Social Security in America. Sluggish European growth is attributed to socialist overregulation, whereas in fact one of the most heavily regulated economies in the EU—Germany—is also the most successful.

None of these countries are actually socialist at all. Some, such as the UK, France, Italy, Spain, and Germany, may have played with socialism in the past, but all have long abandoned that path. Rather, these are in effect mild Authoritarian Right nations that have found a balance between public and private goods—some more successfully than others—as means of repayment of the real selectorate.

Very rarely do right-wingers in this country point to *real* Left Libertarian (or, perhaps, more accurately, Democratic Libertarian) nations. These would include Canada, Denmark, Sweden, Norway, Iceland, the Netherlands, Ireland, Switzerland, and New Zealand—a group of countries that have discovered how to make Democratic Libertarianism work. These are societies where democratic participation is high and the real selectorate large and active, leading to a winning coalition that is wide. Because of this, governments in these countries have to rule by paying back the selectorate through the provision of *public* goods—health care, education, and welfare. They balance expenditures based on the Maslow hierarchy with a compact with their citizenry that finances these expenditures through taxation. They build structures to deliver on these promises but—and it's a big but—where structures, rules, or regulations are not necessary, they mostly leave well enough alone.

Here's the funny thing: The majority of these countries are to be found in the top twenty where GDP per capita is concerned,[8] *and* they occupy *eight* of the top ten countries that are the happiest in the world.[9]

Rich *and* happy? How can that be?

The answer, as we shall see, lies in their firm dedication to true Democratic Libertarianism. But, before laying out what this looks like, there is one final aspect of political society that we have to deal with—and one on which all of these countries score low—and that is ideological absolutism.

---

8   International Monetary Fund, 2017, and World Bank, 2016.
9   United Nations Happiness Report, 2018.

6

The Role of Ideology in Societal Breakdown

S een in the gamut of human history, ideology is a relatively recent phe-nomenon, emerging as a way of making sense of the world during the American and French revolutions. It could be argued that one of the earliest ideologies to emerge into the political limelight was that of the Found-ing Fathers in the Declaration of Independence: "We hold these truths to be self-evident, that all men are created equal, that they are endowed by their Creator with certain inalienable Rights, that among these are Life, Lib-erty and the pursuit of Happiness." Here was a normative set of beliefs (the definition of "ideology") that these men believed should govern the new society they wished to create. These were truly radical and revolutionary concepts—in no major country had there existed the notion before that men were created equal or that the vast majority of them had any "Rights" whatsoever, let alone the pursuit of life, liberty (really?), and the pursuit of happiness (what on earth did that have to do with anything?). There were the ruling classes, who either were blessed with divine right or had come into their positions through choosing the right side in particularly bloody power battles. And there was the rest of humanity. That was just the way things were. Similarly, in France just a few years later, there emerged the ideology of "liberté, egalité, fraternité." Both of these ideologies grew initially from an increasing frustration with the power structures of the time and their effects on the populations under their yokes—in America, taxation without representation, and in France, a devastating famine.

Before this time, however, politics was not really based on ideas. It was based on power and who held it. Some might quarrel with this assessment, pointing to the English Civil War, which pitted king (divine right) against parliament (limited democratic involvement in government). But even there, the underlying theme could be argued to have been religion—a Catholic-leaning king who believed in his divine right just as his Catholic-leaning father had done, versus a Protestant parliament that viewed this as heresy.

Ah, yes, I hear you say, but isn't religion itself ideology? Aren't Christianity and all its component parts ideologies, as well as Islam, Buddhism, Hinduism, and all the rest of them? In a way, you would be right, since all of these are sets of normative beliefs that govern behavior to some extent or another. But they did not necessarily inform the ways in which governments and societies worked. Yes, medieval Europe was a Christian set of lands, but they were hardly run on Christian values. These were not the lands of "love your neighbor as yourself." Even when religions went to war, as they did during the Crusades, the issue was much more about land and power than it was about the religious ideologies of the warring armies (although it did give great cover to those pursuing war). Henry VIII didn't convert England to Protestantism from a deep set of beliefs; he did it in order to divorce his wife and gain control of the riches of the Church.

While it can be argued that religious ideology did play a major role in earlier history, the actual tenets of those ideologies probably had less to do with how society was governed than did the dictates of power and the needs of kings to pay off their very small selectorates. It was not until the eighteenth century that secular ideologies began to emerge that had less to do with religion than with an overarching idea of how society and government should interact.

So, what is "ideology"? According to Willard A. Mullins, a Canadian political scientist writing in the 1970s, an ideology is a set of beliefs that is marked by four characteristics: It must have power over cognition (that is, be so powerful that it supersedes rational thought); it must be capable of guiding one's evaluations; it must provide guidance toward action; and it must be logically coherent (even if it overrides cognition). Karl Marx had another definition, perhaps more succinct and cynical, and here I am going to quote from the New World Encyclopedia:

Marx defined "ideology" as a "false consciousness" of a ruling class in society who falsely present their ideas as if they were universal truth. Their ideas were neither universal nor objective, Marx argued, but they emerged out of and served their class interests.

The supreme irony here, of course, is that Marx's ideas and philosophy were themselves hijacked into an ideology that became known as Marx*ism*. And, just like almost all political ideologies spanning the period from the nineteenth century to today, Marxism became toxic and ultimately destructive.

Whether you take Mullins's or Marx's definition, the key takeaway is that ideology involves people believing in a set of ideas that, even if they are contradicted by fact (cognition), are held fast and lead to actions that may or may not be in society's best interests. Marxism, for example, led to the formation of the Soviet Union and the ultimate slaughter of millions of its citizens. For what? To uphold the ideology or to safeguard power? National Socialism in Germany led to world war and the slaughter of six million Jews and others. Why? Because the ideology was so pure or to uphold power? In

Zimbabwe and Venezuela, socialism led to economic destruction and mass poverty. Again, the ultimate aim was the preservation of power.

Marx may not have gotten many things right, but in this definition he was spot-on. Secular ideology invariably is perverted to serve those who have the most to gain from it, and from there, it leads to destruction. Which is why it is so pernicious in modern-day American society and should be resisted every step of the way. We see it in so many ways, from the fringes (white supremacists, for example) to the mainstream. Both of the major political parties are riven by ideological wars—that is, when they are not warring against each other. Republicans cling to the ideology of minimalist government as if it were a religion, but they cannot agree among each other as to how minimalist "minimalist" should be. Democrats cling to the redemptive power of government, but progressives push this much further than their centrist brethren. The problem here is that ideologies are never right. They never take into account the vast reality of life; they try and simplify it into a trite set of core beliefs that people can relate to (power over cognition), even to the point where they will vote against their own interests. It gets even worse when mixed with religion, as it does on the Evangelical Right. Now you have people who are religious ideologues deciding that they (and they alone) can tell the rest of society how to live, legislate for it through Congress and state legislatures, and interfere with people in their most private lives—all the while espousing minimalist government.

In the United States, ideology is usually associated with specific interest groups, often mixed with tropes of morality, and usually results in some part of society being cast as "others." Often, it is based in documents that are cast as being "absolute"—the Bible or the Constitution, for example—but which are cherry-picked for selective proof of the ideologue's moral superiority.

There are two problems with this:

1. It short-circuits people's ability to think for themselves (cognition) and provides them with an all-too-easy way in which to justify their basic prejudices.

2. It allows for ideologues (whether real or fake) to lead people by dint of a supposed "truth" rather than on the basis of what they really can or cannot do for them.

This makes the American public—much like the Germans and Italians of the 1930s—much more susceptible to the "call" of charismatic leaders, whether good or bad. Some of these lead people to concentrate on their better selves (for example, Martin Luther King, Billy Graham, or even Barack Obama), while others are equally adept at releasing people's inner meanness (Trump, Andrew Jackson, and, sadly, Franklin Graham). The more people feel disenfranchised, the more they lack security, and the more likely they are to follow a charismatic ideological narrative, however good or bad. Unfortunately, this also means that people are willing to follow the ideologue into an authoritarian reality (whether left or right), convinced of the "need" for "strong leadership" and/or all the while being fed a diet of libertarian promises that cannot and will not be kept.

In order to be set free from the siren calls of ideology, America needs to enter into a world in which it is much more difficult for ideological memes to take hold and where government is truly held accountable for what it delivers, not what it promises. At this point, to quote John Lennon, "you may think I am a dreamer" but, as he goes on to say, "I am not the only one." If the good citizens of Scandinavia, Canada, New Zealand, and Switzerland can do this, so can we. It's not easy, and it will never be perfect, but it has been demonstrably proven that it can be done. The secret lies in the word "security."

Life, Liberty, and the Pursuit of Happiness

The American dream is in danger of disappearing

Our system of government is breaking down, our society is fragmenting, and the United States is becoming exceptional in ways that we don't want. We have become a "flawed" democracy.

It's time to return to first principles: the Constitution.

We can do this through recognizing the need for change and by implementing that change based on the interaction of three fundamental frameworks:

MASLOW'S HIERARCHY

The fundamentals for living a fulfilled life based in the key concept of security.
Securitas: absence of fear

EMBEDDING DEMOCRACY

Realize and plan for the cynicism on which politics is based. Ensure that the "winning coalition" is as broad as possible.

DEMOCRATIC LIBERTARIANISM

Government and society that lays the frameworks of freedom and security—and then gets out of the way.

Democratic Libertarian countries are wealthier, more peaceful, and happier.

PART TWO

Security: A Fundamental Right

7

Security: A Social Contract

Let's imagine we all live in a world that defines the lower left-hand quadrant of our simple political map from Chapter 5. Instead of calling this Left Libertarianism (which smacks too much of ideology), let's call it Democratic Libertarian or Free Democracy. In this world, there is a simple but overarching and compelling contract: Everybody has the right to live in a free, secure world in return for payment of taxes and real involvement in the community at its most granular level. Ten descriptors define this world:

1. It is *libertarian*, not authoritarian. At the center of this world is the right to live in freedom, with a minimum of unnecessary rules and regulations decided by others. Those rules and regulations that do exist do so for the benefit of all members of society (or, at least, the largest majority possible) and not for the enrichment of small groups.

2. It is *inclusive*, not exclusive. Nobody in this society cares whether you are black or white, gay or straight, Jewish or Muslim, artist or laborer, male or female. You are taken at face value for who you are.

3. It is *empathetic*, not sympathetic. In the wake of the recent spate of school

shootings in America, there has been something of a backlash at those politicians and groups who routinely state that the community involved is "in our thoughts and prayers." Thoughts and prayers mean that I am thinking about you and praying for you, but I am not actually feeling what you are feeling, and worse, I am not doing anything about it. In an empathetic society, people not only feel others' sorrows (as well as their joys) but get together and do something about it.

4. It is based in *community*, not the absolute rule of the majority over the minority. Yes, there have to be laws, and yes, they need to be obeyed. But they should be laws agreed to in community, not based on an authoritarian idea of obedience out of fear of punishment. People "of a certain age" can remember back to a time when police would take a young miscreant back to his or her parents to face their wrath rather than arrest them, humiliate them, and drag them through the courts, only then to be incarcerated. The United States imprisons a far greater percentage of its population than does any other civilized nation on earth. It's a massive waste and a self-fulfilling system that perpetuates crime and poverty rather than seeking to cure it. A Free Democracy relies on the community to get to the root of such issues—and, indeed, provides the security in which the need or temptation to resort to crime is greatly reduced.

5. It is *supportive,* not suppressive. Authoritarian societies seek to suppress certain types of behavior—and, in some cases, certain types of people—and, in the case of America, often declares "war" on them. We have the war on drugs, the war on crime, the war on immigration. A society that thinks like this acts like it. Before long, its police forces are militarized units, engaged in war, and often seen as occupying armies. This is in direct contradiction to what we see written on police cars in so many cities: "To Protect and Serve." Free Democratic societies actually believe in that slogan and put it into practice. There's a reason British police don't carry guns—they are there as supportive resources who are on your side, not as your suppressor.

6. It is *respectful*, not disrespectful. In a Free Democracy, every neighbor is as important as you are and as everyone else is. They treat each other with respect. This, perhaps, without getting overly religious or dogmatic, is the living embodiment of "love your neighbor as yourself." It is certainly not a society in which the president routinely spews out disrespect on Twitter on a daily basis. In a Free Democratic world, leadership at that level is servant leadership, where the president and Congress are there truly to serve the interests of the nation.

7. It is a *listening*, not a telling, society. Far too often today, we are told what to think. Politicians, lobbyists, talking heads on TV and radio—they all seem to be fixated on telling us what is good for us, not listening to us. Some of the best journalists today (for example, Christiane Amanpour) are inveterate listeners. What they constantly tell us is that people, whether in America or elsewhere, share many of the same frustrations and aspirations, whether liberal or conservative, black or white, old or young. If they listened to one another, they would find this out and realize just how hollow the ideologues really are.

8. It is a *patriotic* society, not a nationalistic one. As Tim Marshall famously said, "Respect for your own and respect for others is patriotism. Respect for your own and complete disrespect for others is nationalism." America has much to be proud of but it also has a lot to admire in other nations and societies. A Free Democratic America would do so without reservation and without chest-thumping.

9. It is an *inspirational* society, not a fearful one. It is a terrible thing for a child to be afraid to go to school when in fact they are looking for inspiration as to what to do with their lives. America has a long history of inspiration—just witness all its Nobel Prize winners; its achievements in science, medicine, and space; and its artistic prowess. A society living in fear cannot find—or continue to find—inspiration. The environment for inspiration has to be there.

10. Above all, it is a *secure* society, where security is present in all its Maslovian dimensions. Insecurity, at any of Maslow's levels, is corrosive and destructive. It allows for the creeping introduction of corruption and the spurious justification of authoritarian structures and policies. Security has to be at the center of a Free Democratic society, its guiding principle and its bedrock.

In a Free Democratic—or Democratic Libertarian—world, security is defined as an environment in which Maslow's hierarchy is fully delivered without the burdens of excessive regulation or the oppressive rule of law. Let's reprise what this means in reality:

SELF-
ACTUALIZATION
morality, creativity,
spontaneity, acceptance,
experience purpose, meaning,
and inner potential

SELF-ESTEEM
confidence, achievement, respect for
others, the need to be a unique indiviual

LOVE AND BELONGING
friendship, family, intimacy, sense of connection

SAFETY AND SECURITY
health, employment, property, family, and social ability

PHYSIOLOGICAL NEEDS
breathing, food, water, shelter, clothing, sleep

Maslow's Hierarchy of Needs

Physiological security is the basic premise on which a society survives and thrives. It is the community's promise to each individual that they shall have enough to eat, a safe environment for now and the future, and somewhere to rest their head.

Safety is the framework within which we can deliver on this basic premise. It comprises the following:

- *National security*—that is, a defense capability that is sufficient to safeguard the country and its interests, but no more

- *Personal security*—law enforcement based on protecting me, the citizen, not the state

- *Financial security*—an economic system that provides for sustainable growth such that I, the citizen, can feel confident in my ability to provide for myself and my family now and in the future, and that allows me to share equitably in the wealth that is generated

- *Educational security*—the universal provision of high-quality education that will enable me to gain financial security, build my esteem, and allow me to self-actualize

- *Health security*—recognition that health is a societal investment that enables financial security, reduces societal cost, and affords me the ability to build again if I become affected by sickness

- *Environmental security*—strongly linked to both national and health security, and of increasing importance and urgency, is the need to counteract the forces of nature being unleashed upon this planet before they completely change the world in which we live for the worse

Each of these is a national investment provided through the contract by our payment of taxes but one which we expect our governments to facilitate (if not provide outright) to its utmost in order to provide a secure environment in which to live. Failure to do so, on any level, is a betrayal of the contract.

Belonging in the context of society and government is founded in the freedom to associate with whom I please, as long as it does not impinge on the security of others. It allows me the ability to build community and participate in society. From government's point of view, it is the provision of a framework and a level playing field in and on which my contribution can count as much as that of any other citizen. It is about feeling included, and its ultimate expression is that of citizenship.

Which leads us to *esteem*. By this we do not mean self-puffery but the fact that I, as a citizen, matter. It does not matter whether I am white, black, Latino, Asian, or Native American; male or female; Protestant, Muslim, Jewish, or Catholic; straight or gay. All that matters is that I am a citizen. I am part of the winning coalition because I am a citizen. I, the citizen, am part of the reason why this is an exceptional and successful country. With the security of citizenship, I am part of the whole and worthy of respect, while respecting others. I also recognize that others aspire to this status, and I encourage and welcome them into the fold because I know that, in allowing them the same esteem that I have, they will contribute to the future security and success of this nation. With the security of citizenship, they and I are laying down the foundation for the future.

Finally, there is *self-actualization*. With physiological, financial, educational, and health security in a society in which I belong and in which I find and give esteem, I am able to reach for the highest and best that I can be. This is hugely important because it allows me to contribute in any way I want—I don't have to be a financially contributing widget in the economy. I can be an artist, a musician, an educator, an environmentalist, or an entrepreneur, or whatever it is that I am supremely good at. And I can do it in an atmosphere that is supportive, fair, and secure while still allowing for economic growth and free markets. This is the ingenuity of America. And I can be a part of that.

This is, in essence, what a Democratic Libertarian society should strive for. It opens the selectorate—and therefore the winning coalition—as wide as possible while providing a framework in which Maslovian security is enabled from bottom to top. But, many would say, you can't call this libertarian—there's too much government involvement in providing this framework. Libertarians believe, after all, that government should provide the very basics and then get out of the way. And, indeed, that may be one definition of libertarianism—you get the basics, after which everybody's destiny is up to themselves and no one else.

I once had a conversation with a barman in Corvallis, Oregon, who espoused this mode of thinking. We were speaking about Obamacare and he was outraged—just outraged—that he should be required to buy health insurance. "But what about," I asked, "if you were hit by a car in the middle of the street and were lying there unconscious and possibly in danger for your life?"

"Leave me to die," he responded. But the fact is that nobody would leave him to die. That's not how civilized societies work. He would be picked up by ambulance, transported to the nearest emergency hospital, and given medical care aimed at saving his life and restoring him to functionality. And that costs. Who pays? The taxpayer and those of us actually paying for insurance. This person, therefore, was implicitly expecting others to pick up the tab for him (even if his bluster said otherwise). That's not libertarian. That's sponging.

That's why a Democratic Libertarian (or Free Democratic) society does not necessarily build itself. There will always be a section of society content to allow others to shoulder the costs of their existence. A Free Democratic society requires leadership—and not just any old leadership or authoritarian leadership, but truly inspirational leadership—to build its frameworks but at the same time allow the liberty and degrees of freedom in which to thrive and succeed.

I had the privilege of being a CEO for more than eighteen years. I also twice led a national trade association. And, in fourteen years of consulting, I have counseled well over one hundred CEOs in their jobs. I have seen leadership in all its guises, from downright awful to truly inspirational. I have met leaders who bordered on (if not crossed the line) of being sociopathic, and I have seen people who have built companies that were extraordinary and whose employees worshipped them. What made the difference? What made a leader truly extraordinary and inspirational? *Forbes*, the bible of management and wealth, talks of the seven secrets of inspirational leaders:

1. They are passionate about what they believe and what they are doing.
2. They have vision.
3. They are engaged with those that they lead on a human level.
4. They paint a picture of where they want to lead you.
5. They invite your participation.
6. They reinforce optimism.
7. They encourage potential.

If we were to think back on the presidents of the last half century or more, there are probably only three who fully meet this definition—Kennedy, Reagan, and Clinton. But these seven traits, in my experience, are not the full measure of inspirational leadership behavior. I believe that such a leader needs honesty and integrity, empathy, discipline and drive, humility, openness, creativeness, self-confidence, and a sense of humor. All of this wraps up into one word that is tremendously important to the young of today: *authenticity*.

In a Free Democratic world, then, an authentic leader would believe strongly not only in the frameworks suggested by the Maslow hierarchy but also in the absolute need to ensure a wide and expanding winning coalition. He or she would have a passion, in other words, for the democratic underpinnings of the country and for the liberty that this implies and protects. That applies not only to federal leadership but also at the state level and in cities, counties, and municipalities.

That there have been and are today such people is indisputable. But, to be honest, they are not that numerous. The American system is too broken by ideology and money to afford success to the passionate and unsullied who want to bring us back to a Free Democratic state. Finding our next Martin Luther King, Nelson Mandela, or Mahatma Ghandi is not going to be easy. Yet maybe there is hope—more women than ever before are running for office, younger generations are far less accepting of hubris (or lack of authenticity) than their parents were, and there is a hunger for principled leadership of the type presently being shown by Bishop Michael Curry, for example.

All of which is to say that the achievement of a Free Democratic society will not come about without leadership and without a strong response from the wider selectorate to that leadership. The American Revolution did not come about without such a combination, nor will the revolution that we need today. But it is not inconceivable, especially if we remember that a Free Democratic contract will depend on three things:

1. A true understanding of how government, society, and the Maslow hierarchy interact

2. A commitment to ensuring that the selectorate—and therefore the winning coalition—is as wide as possible

3. Recognition that Democratic Libertarianism has worked in other parts of the world, all of which are not only rich but happy

This last is extremely important, as the knee-jerk tendency in this country is to label anything in the bottom left-hand quadrant of our political map as "socialism," thereby demonizing it straight out of the gate. This is a call for real conversation about what Democratic Libertarianism *really* means, why it is the way forward, and how we could make it happen.

So, how can we make it happen? What would such a society look like?

What Is
Democratic Libertarianism?

· Libertarian	· Authoritarian
· Inclusive	· Exclusive
· Empathetic	· Sympathetic
· Community-based	· Rule-of-law-based
· Supportive	· Suppressive
· Respectful	· Disrespectful
· Listening	· Telling
· Patriotic	· Nationalistic
· Inspirational	· Fearful
· Secure	· Insecure

GOVERNMENT OF THE PEOPLE,
BY THE PEOPLE,
FOR THE PEOPLE.

8

The Basics: Physiological Security

Physiological security—the basic premise that is the community's promise to each individual that they shall have enough to eat, a safe environment for now and the future, and somewhere to rest their head.

Why is physiological security important? Surely, in a libertarian society, isn't it pretty much everyone for themselves? After all, did not Margaret Thatcher famously opine that "there is no such thing as society"? And were not she and Ronald Reagan in lockstep on this during a period of great economic growth when "greed was good"? Yes, indeed. And what happened next? Black Friday and the recession of the early nineties, resulting in the election in the United States of Bill Clinton on the simple message, "It's the economy, stupid."

The simple truth is that a society that cannot provide physiological security has no basis for survival. A society that ignores the things that bind it will fall, while one that treasures those things will usually survive. In America's recent history, we only have to look at the Great Depression for evidence. The Hoover administration viewed the likely effects of the 1929 Crash more from a financial point of view than a humanistic one. Thus, there was more emphasis on the federal budget than there was on humanitarian aid, with Hoover opposing direct federal relief efforts until late into his tenure. That—and the disastrous passage of the Smoot-Hawley Tariff legislation that restricted international trade—sent markets, industries, and agriculture spiraling and resulted in an unemployment rate of 25 percent. Had the physiological security of the citizenry been foremost in the government's mind at that time (as it was to a greater degree in 2008), the devastating effects of the Great Depression on vast numbers of individuals in society would have been greatly mitigated.

The really stupid thing about societies putting financial or corporate needs ahead of human physiological ones—a real Simpson "Doh!"—is that the long-term costs to society and government as a whole are much, much greater. Take, for example, the current US system of paying for health care. By making this an optional opt-in system operated primarily by private insurance companies (with the exceptions of Medicare, Medicaid, and the VA), the system allows between twenty million and thirty million (depending on where we are with Obamacare) to remain uninsured. Even some of those who are insured have policies that place limits on what they can actually claim in the event of catastrophic illness. All of this leads to extreme economic distress for many who encounter major health events, ultimately leading to bankruptcy. The cost to society lies not only in the unpaid medical bills but also in the higher insurance premiums that the insured pay so policy issuers can hedge their bets against this happening. These higher premiums reduce real expendable income and therefore slow the economy down. Medical costs themselves increase as a hedge against nonpayment, while future employers of the bankrupt are less likely to hire them due to their financial circumstances. In each and every instance, society as a whole suffers.

Let's take an example that is close to home in the modern era: the opioid crisis. Since 2001, the opioid epidemic has cost this country over $1 *trillion*, according to the nonprofit group Altarum, which studied CDC mortality data. What's more, they estimate that it will cost us another $500 billion in the next three years alone. These losses are primarily to be found in lost earnings, lost productivity to employers, and tax costs at all levels of government. The late Alan Krueger, a Princeton economist, calculated that opioids account for 43 percent of the observed decline in male labor force participation. A recent study by the University of North Carolina at Chapel Hill found the same phenomenon *and* that there is an increase in investment in labor-saving technology in areas where opioids are prevalent.[10]

In one way or another, we all lose as a result of this catastrophe. But why did it happen in the first place? Primarily because government, employers, and the "market" as a whole paid scant attention to the human costs of the loss of factories and their well-paying jobs all across the interior of the United States. Instead of there being a safety net for the workers and their families who suddenly found themselves living in cities and towns with few to no jobs, they were pretty much left to their own devices. Without income, they lost their homes, their health insurance, their local tax bases, their schools, and local businesses. Inevitably, all of this led to despair, and despair led them to activities that would dull the pain. While there were some halfhearted attempts to provide "retraining" for these workers, it wasn't much good if there weren't the employers there to take advantage of their new skills. Interestingly enough, there *was* a group in Congress that looked carefully into possible programs for providing even more help to people in these transition areas—specific welfare grants, relocation help—especially where steel plants were closing. They were persuaded, however, by the steel industry itself not to do this for fear it would undermine the industry's attempts to push the government into imposing tariffs on imported steel. If they helped workers who had lost their jobs, so the argument went, they

---

10   "The Impact of the Opioid Crisis on Firm Value and Investment." UNC–Chapel Hill Kenan-Flagler Business School, 2019.

would be admitting that they were closing plants and so could not make the case for tariffs to keep those same plants open. Kafka would have had a ball with that one.

Out of this type of "market" thinking has come both the opioid crisis and the election of Donald Trump. Had those in government abided by their duty to honor their most basic duty—to provide for the physiological security of the people—it is arguable that neither of these things would have happened. Governments in some of the more democratic countries around the world do indeed have policies of supporting laid-off workers not only with retraining but with minimum income payments and even, in some cases, relocation assistance. Their thinking is clear—getting people back into good-paying jobs as fast as possible is a lot cheaper than paying out welfare, picking up the costs of unhealthy living, and having people be unproductive.

A related and equally pernicious crisis facing both the US and the UK today is that of mental health and homelessness. The reason why it exists in both these countries but less so in other developed nations goes back thirty years, when Reagan and Thatcher (who were ideological soul mates) decided that mental illness should be dealt with "in the community." In 1980, the Carter administration passed a landmark piece of legislation called the Mental Health Systems Act (MHSA), which laid down a framework for federal support and financing for local mental health community centers and provided for coordination of mental health with general health care and social support services. In 1981, under President Reagan, this legislation was repealed, and the whole issue of mental health was punted to the states. As a result, mental health institutions started to close, and it became the mantra that the mentally ill should be cared for by their local communities (who, of course, had scarce resources to do so). Thatcher did pretty much the same in Britain. The mentally ill were left to determine their own fates—something that, by definition, many of them could not do. Fast-forward to today and one-third of the homeless living on American streets have mental health issues while no less than half of those in our jails are also mentally ill. In essence, we shoved the problem onto the streets and then into the jails.

Once again, government failed in its primary duty—to provide for the physiological security of people not able to help themselves. Once again, the cost to society is enormous. Lost productivity due to mental illness costs the United States $193 billion a year,[11] and that does not even take into account the cost to local taxpayers of the strain on their law enforcement and incarceration systems. In America, there is an even more insidious cost: that of mentally ill people gaining access to lethal weapons and embarking on massacres in schools; shopping malls; places of work; and places, such as Las Vegas, where large crowds gather. Given government's historic role in exacerbating the problem of mental illness in society, it is stomach-roiling to hear politicians of all stripes beat their chests about the lack of mental health intervention to prevent such attacks.

The United States is the most charitable nation in the world, bar none. Americans give around 1.4 percent of the GDP to charity every year[12]— almost double that of the next most giving nation, New Zealand. I don't know about you, but my mailbox is routinely stuffed with begging letters from charities every day. I probably get twenty such letters a week. And, yes, I give. But should we be patting ourselves on the back for this? Isn't it instead a symptom of the fact that we have so many physiological security issues in this country (health, mental illness, homelessness) that the need for these charities abounds? If society as a whole were putting physiological security at the forefront of its existence, and using its tax dollars to do so, would we need them? Hard-line libertarians (i.e., those more oriented to the right of our quadrants) might say that this is precisely what ought to hap-pen—government should stay out of these things, and the local community should, if it so wishes, step in. But here is the awkward truth: The Charities

---

11   National Alliance on Mental Illness, 2019.
12   Charities Aid Foundation.

Aid Foundation, in its study of giving around the world, found there was no correlation whatsoever between the levels of taxation in a country and the charitable generosity of its people. Which leads us to believe that it is *what government spends its tax dollars on* that makes the difference. If you are spending 50 percent of your budget on defense, there is far less to spend on basic physiological needs. If your defense spending is more in line with what is actually needed to defend your country (rather than police the world), there is rather more to spend on those basic needs and a lesser requirement to depend on charity. This leads us to a rather more complex argument about defense spending, which we will tackle later on. The basic question here for the moment is this: We are all spending a large amount of our take-home pay on taxation, so given Maslow's hierarchy of needs, should we not be entitled to think that our governments (at all levels) should be concerned with providing for our most basic physiological security?

Finally, while we are on the subject of physiological security, let's talk about the environment. In 2014, the state-appointed emergency manager of Flint, Michigan—a man named Michael Brown—and his team decided to switch Flint's water supply from the Detroit Water and Sewerage Department (which sourced and treated its water from Lake Huron) to the Flint River. The reason was simple—Flint was experiencing an economic crisis, and this was one way to reduce costs. However, as the switchover occurred, local officials failed to turn on corrosion inhibitors that would have kept the water safe from corroding lead pipes. As a result, lead leached into the drinking water at a level that well exceeded federal safety margins, leading to between 6,000 and 12,000 children being exposed to severe health damage caused by the water they were drinking. Despite being apprised of this disaster in late 2014, those in control of Flint (including its emergency manager and mayor) persisted in denying there was a problem for over a year, exacerbating the health crisis faced by the city's residents. Once again, money trumped humanitarian concerns until the problem became catastrophic. Once again, government (this time local and state) failed in its duty to provide physiological security.

Flint provided a microcosmic glimpse of an environmental battle that has been going on for decades in the United States. Sadly, the contours of the battle are well known and highly repetitive. Science provides evidence of environmental degradation, whether that be pollution from coal-burning power plants, global warming, water security, or environmental pollution from various modes of transport. Responsive governments propose and enact rules and regulations to try and mitigate such degradation. (Note that I said "responsive" governments, not democratic ones. It was, after all, Nixon that established the Environmental Protection Agency by executive order in 1970.) Those with financial stakes in polluting industries argue with all their might and as many alternative facts as they can that they are not to blame and that rules and regulations harm the economy. Nonresponsive governments roll the rules back, and the cycle begins again. Sadly, the Trump government, aware of its base in areas such as West Virginia, has taken the cycle and enhanced it, withdrawing from the Paris climate agreement on the basis that the accord damaged the American economy. To be fair, Trump may feel that he is responding to the physiological security needs of all of those in coal and steel country who need their jobs back, but the ultimate truth is that he is risking another key element of physiological security—the need to live in a nontoxic environment and one in which we are not exposed to rising sea levels, extreme weather patterns, and ecological disaster.

In the end, money once again trumps government's duty to provide physiological security, and the ultimate costs to society will eventually be much higher than had humanitarian physiological needs been pushed to the forefront of policy-making.

These are but a few examples of short-term, market-based thinking undermining the most basic duties of a society and its government to provide a framework in which we can all have food, have a roof over our heads, and live in environmental safety. But, you will be asking, how would a Democratic Libertarian society and government do any of this any differently?

Let's start with the basic premise: *In a Democratic Libertarian environment, no citizen will be denied their basic right to security where food, health, housing, or environment is concerned.*

I can hear the cries of indignation from the Authoritarian Right now: "Socialism!" "Welfare state!" "Government dependence!" To which I would respond, "Are Canada or New Zealand socialist states?" "Is Norway a welfare state?" "Do Danes depend on their government?" The answers to which are a simple "no." And let's not forget that these are the nations that are the happiest on this planet, as well as among the richest. So, let's see how the United States could achieve the same elevated status.

Physiological security is the most basic of needs in the Maslow hierarchy. If we are to have "government of the people, by the people, for the people" and if "the proposition that all men are created equal" is really true, as Lincoln so famously said, then denying that security "even unto the least of us" is to deny the ethos of why the United States exists and why it should continue to exist. The challenge is how to provide that security without interfering with the unique capability of Americans to innovate, produce, and lead.

To understand how Democratic Libertarianism differs from its counterparts—and why it would behoove the Democratic Party to adopt it—we need to parse Lincoln's iconic phrase a little further. The *Authoritarian Right* are very much about government *of* the people, but less so *by* or *for*. Witness their repeated attempts to suppress the voting rights and capabilities of blacks and their unwavering support of business over the rights of the individual. The *Authoritarian Left* has never really gained ground in the US, but where it has elsewhere in the world, it has always started out as *by* and *for* and then gravitated almost exclusively to *of*. The fantasy world of the *Libertarian Right*, pushed by so many Republicans running for power until they actually get there, is built around the mantra "What government? We don't need government!" Which leaves the *Libertarian Left* (what we are calling "Democratic Libertarians") to fulfill Lincoln's vision to its fullest: *of*, *by*, and *for*.

In a Democratic Libertarian society, there is no excuse for any single human being in this great and wealthy country going without food or shelter. Many of us live in cities or towns where the homeless are to be found panhandling on streets, outside supermarkets, or at the intersections of major highways. Many of these, shamefully, are veterans. Many suffer from PTSD. Many suffer from mental illness. If you take the time to engage with these individuals (which, sadly, many of us don't), you will discover that very few of them want to be homeless. Yes, there are those who prefer to be outside society, but they are a distinct minority. Most are there because, in some way or another, society failed them. They were felled by a major illness, lost their jobs, lost their insurance, lost their homes. A quarter of them have mental illnesses for which they cannot get treatment. Some had decent homes that they rented, but then their landlords sold up, and the new owners raised the rents so high that they were forced out—sometimes at the point of eviction. Some fell victim to drug or alcohol addiction. Others lost their livelihoods through divorce. The stories are legion, but the underlying theme is that there was no safety net to catch them.

A Democratic Libertarian society would provide that safety net at three levels:

1. It would mitigate the causes of homelessness and hunger.

2. It would provide resources for rehabilitation for those who find themselves homeless.

3. It would facilitate their reentry into society as productive and proud members of that society.

Let's look at these one at a time. First, how would such a society mitigate the causes of homelessness and hunger? There are many more qualified than I to analyze these causes in detail, so I shall rely here on the work done by the National Law Center on Homelessness and Poverty (NLCHP). Their findings divide causes for homelessness into those that force families to lose their homes and those that force individuals to do so.

FAMILIIES	INDIVIDUALS
Lack of affordable housing	Lack of affordable housing
Unemployment	Unemployment
Poverty	Poverty
Low wages	Mental illness
	Substance abuse

In addition to these, among women a major cause was domestic abuse.

Unemployment, poverty, and low wages form part of the bedrock of the problem, but it can often be an unrelated trigger that forces either the family or the individual over the edge. These can include divorce, domestic abuse, loss of a job, or a death in the family. In some instances, it is the removal of housing affordability through increases in rent or eviction. One of the crises facing Raleigh, North Carolina, right now, for example, is the gentrification of many neighborhoods where new landlords are buying up properties, forcing tenants out, and then redeveloping for an altogether different demographic. Raleigh is by no means alone in this.

Where mental illness and substance abuse are concerned, the NLCHP adds a very important rider: "and the lack of needed services." At any one time in the United States there are three million people who are homeless (not including those bunking up with relatives or friends), and over a third of these are children. The cost to society in terms of lost productivity and temporary services is significant—but to the individuals and families so afflicted, massive. So how does a Democratic Libertarian society not only deal with this but prevent it, thus reducing the burden on all concerned?

The first issue to deal with is that of affordable housing. In communities successfully addressing this, the problem is tackled at two levels. The first deals with the need for affordable housing *now* for the existing homeless. Experience has shown that deliberately building new or converting existing housing for the use of homeless families and individuals lifts these people into a position where they can devote their resources to finding jobs, building income, and finding security. As they do so, they rely less on government or charity and become contributory members of society once again.

The second level is much more strategic, which is deliberately to ensure that, amid all the private development of neighborhoods, there is also a plan for housing that is either publicly or, more usually, publicly and privately financed and is truly affordable for those who need it the most. Realizing that it faced a situation in which 150,000 people would not be able to afford homes by the end of the decade, Wake County (incorporating Raleigh) embarked on a twenty-year plan to build affordable housing for all its citizens.

This is civic government at its best, realizing that investment in basic human security now means much lower costs in the future as well as a population that is productive and happy. Encouragement for such investments from both federal and state governments would propel us to a society where homelessness was considerably reduced. Through addressing the first issue— how do we mitigate the problem?—and drilling down to primary causes, we are able to both rehabilitate those whom the system failed and bring them back to productivity and self-sufficiency.

Let's now look at hunger and poverty. In 2016, there were 40.6 million people in the United States living in poverty—or 12.7 percent of the population.[13] That's more than one in eight of the entire population. Granted, as the economy has improved and unemployment has fallen, that figure has been steadily declining since its Great Recession peak and has probably receded further at the time of this writing. Nevertheless, this is the richest country in the world, and we still have more than one in ten living in poverty? Not only that, but just under twenty million Americans live in *extreme* poverty—that is, with incomes of $10,000 a year or less for a family of four. Worse, this scourge is not evenly distributed. In the same year, 24.1

---

13   World Hunger Education Service 2018, quoting United States Census Bureau.

percent of blacks and 21.4 percent of Hispanics were living below the official poverty line—one in four blacks and one in five Hispanics. In 2015, 12.7 percent of US households suffered from "food insecurity" (since 2006, government-speak for hunger). In Mississippi, that percentage was 20.8 percent, or one-fifth of that state's population. How does the Mississippi legislature or governor sleep at night knowing that they are failing a fifth of their people?

But let's also be fair here. There are government programs in place that do actually reduce the overall rates of hunger and poverty. These include SNAP (also known as food stamps), which helped forty-five million people in 2015; WIC, which targets nutrition for women and children; and the National School Lunch Program, which helps more than twenty million children each day with free or reduced-cost lunches. These all cost money at both the federal and state level. But they need not do so, for the simple reason that if employees in a supposedly full-employment economy were receiving living wages, they would not need to resort to government welfare. This is a prime example of where Democratic Libertarianism works better than the Authoritarian Right: If society set a living minimum wage, government could actually get out of the way in terms of having to administer, at taxpayer expense, programs to mitigate the effects of its own neglect. More than seven million Americans work two or more jobs, not because they are wonderful entrepreneurs but because the jobs they actually do have don't pay them enough to survive or to feed their families. If their primary job paid them enough, that would mean they would have more time for their kids, more time to care for their families, and less need to revert to government programs.

Opponents of a living minimum wage inevitably argue that the higher costs to employers would mean less people employed, more unemployment, and businesses less able to compete. According to them, paying people $7.25 an hour (a figure that has not changed since 2009) is actually good for the economy. That equates to an annual salary of $14,500 a year. The government's own definition of poverty for a family of four is an annual household income of less than $24,600 a year. No wonder people are working two jobs.

However, let's dig a little deeper here and admit to some facts. In 2013, economists Jonathan Meer and Jeremy West found that raising the minimum wage did not reduce employment but that it did slow job growth in those states that raised it above the federal floor.[14] So, does this mean that raising the minimum wage is necessarily a bad thing if it slows economic growth? The answer to that is a most definitive no. Here's why. Economics is always about achieving equilibrium. If the economy expands too fast, beyond the ability of available resources to sustain that growth, it will eventually contract. If the contraction goes too far and interest rates and wages fall, capital will start to flow in again and it will expand. There is always a search for equilibrium, *but equilibrium never happens.* If we raise the living minimum wage and job growth slows, the economy will adjust and seek a new equilibrium until such time as demand adjusts to new pricing levels and starts to pick up again. The economy is not a zero-sum game, nor is it fixed in a moment in time. It is a journey, the direction of which is determined by a myriad of different inputs, only one of which is the wages of those at the bottom of the pile.

Consider, for a moment, Henry Ford. Not only did he conceive of a popular and revolutionary mode of transport (the Model T) but he also invented mass production. But then he needed a market for all the cars he was producing. So he took the crazy step of increasing the wages of his workers to $5 a day—an insane amount for the time in which he lived. His idea was that if you paid your workers well, they could afford your products. Similarly, while raising the living minimum wage would temporarily slow job growth, the people receiving that wage would have more money to spend, raise demand, and reduce their dependence on the government. The equilibrium would have been reset.

The skeptical among you might now say, "That's a nice theory, but where's the proof?" Well, let's go back to those rich, democratic left, happy

---

14   National Bureau of Economic Research working paper no. 19262.

countries we encountered earlier. Among the economies measured by the World Economic Forum, the Netherlands, New Zealand, Ireland, and Canada all have higher minimum wages than the United States does. By other measures, Denmark has the highest of them all. Yet these are all countries that not only compete well on the global market but have attained wealth and happiness. All also have the widest selectorates in the world. In other words, governments are having to use public goods (a high minimum wage) to pay their winning coalitions and are reaping the benefits.

But wages are not the only determinant of poverty and hunger. We saw earlier that, among individuals, substance abuse was one of the primary causes of homelessness and that poverty and hunger afflict the black and Hispanic populations more than any other. Poverty is also much more prevalent among single-parent families. It will not surprise you that these three statistics are heavily correlated. Black families are more likely to be single-parent; substance abuse afflicts this population more than others; and the rate of incarceration among black men is far higher than among other segments as a result, which leads right back to the prevalence of single-parent households. That this should be so is directly correlated to the war on drugs started by Nixon and amplified by Reagan. While the US population grew by 51 percent between 1974 and 2014, the number of people incarcerated over that time increased by no less than 600 percent.[15] What's more, while there is evidence to suggest that white people consume and sell drugs at the same rate as do blacks and Hispanics, they are far less likely to be imprisoned for their infractions. Making up 30 percent of the overall population, blacks and Hispanics make up 53 percent of the prison population. The majority of these are men, leaving women to bring up families alone while being the sole breadwinner. What's more, America imprisons far more of its people than virtually any other country in the world. We make up 4.4 percent of the globe's population and yet account for 22 percent of its prisoners. In response

---

15 "Criminal Justice Facts," The Sentencing Project, 2018.

to this, an entire industry of privately run prisons to which the states out-source their criminal populations has been born.

The story that the math tells is both breathtaking and heartbreaking. By waging a "war" on drugs disproportionately against minorities and the poor, we have created an underclass that is condemned to continue living in poverty and that costs the country a fortune in incarceration, let alone benefits such as SNAP and WIC. What's more, we have already seen in the opioid crisis that drug usage is often the last resort of the despairing. So, when faced with overwhelming odds, the likelihood is that people of whatever color will both seek out and sell drugs. Karl Marx wrote, "Religion is the opium of the masses." He was wrong. Drugs themselves are the opium of the despairing masses.

Here is a prime example of where libertarianism actually gets it right. Because of continuing government interference and draconian policies, entire populations and generations have been destroyed at an enormous financial and social cost. It would have been far better for government to have removed the causes of both the demand and the supply of dangerous drugs into the market. Mexican drug cartels and Chinese fentanyl factories would not make such enormous profits were not the drugs in question illegal and therefore more expensive than they would ever be under a regulated but legal regime. There is very little difference between the situation with drugs today and alcohol in the Prohibition era. Restrict and criminalize supply when demand is strong and you drive prices up, making it all the more attractive to organized crime to get involved. The mob needs street mules, and so even more people enter into criminal life. They get nabbed under a government-declared "war," the incarceration rate goes up, costs soar, and families are thrown onto the scrap heap. Meanwhile, more and more drug users die. Is this providing for physiological security?

Where pure libertarianism gets it wrong is to suggest that we merely legalize drug usage and get the hell out of the way. That's like placing no restrictions at all on alcohol or tobacco usage and wondering why we have a generation of alcoholic, chain-smoking schoolchildren. By contrast, under Democratic Libertarianism, there is a recognition that some boundaries have to be set in order to enable the very security that is government's primary responsibility. Gangs of drunken teenagers roaming the streets would not provide security for the rest of the population, nor would it reduce the costs on society when these same children end up in the hospital as a result of their drinking. The same applies to drugs.

Not all drugs are created equal. Marijuana usage has not been shown to lead to serious societal or health issues (indeed, it is being used to help in certain medical situations), even where it has been legalized for recreational use. The last time I went to Amsterdam, for example, where marijuana is sold openly in coffee shops, I did not find a modern equivalent of Sodom and Gomorrah or a city in the midst of collapse. In a recent Pew poll, 61 percent of the American population favor legalizing the drug, viewing it in much the same light as alcohol.

Heroin and fentanyl are deadly, though, with deaths from overdoses and illegally "cut" drugs skyrocketing over the last decade. How to control for these differences? A society that seeks to provide physiological security for all cannot just let fentanyl be sold openly and legally without boundaries, but it can create the circumstances in which the drug itself is no longer attractive. Imagine a system in which government-owned drug stores (equivalent to the liquor stores found in some states) sold surrogate drugs and antidotes. Some would be available by prescription; others would be sold over the counter. If these drugs were priced reasonably, such stores would suck the profitability out of the market for the vast majority of drugs, not only from the Chinese and cartels but also from the local meth labs bubbling away in people's bathtubs. The oxygen would be taken out of the whole illegal system. Then imagine that state governments were to set up drug rehab facilities and programs in which users/addicts could enroll under the agreement that they would pay back their treatment through volunteer work, both in the facilities themselves and on the streets. Such programs already exist in the charity sector—imagine what they could do if they were taken on by the states themselves.

Let's work this through. Decriminalizing drugs and making surrogates legally available takes the profit out of the industry and so chokes off supply. State-run rehab facilities wean people off their addictions and boost volunteerism to further reduce usage in the community. Fewer people are arrested, lowering local jail and court costs. Fewer people are convicted, lowering the prison population and all the costs associated with incarcerating so many felons. Families are kept together with two wage earners instead of one, and an entire underclass is lifted out of poverty. Fantasy? No! This is exactly what Portugal did in 2001, and since then rates of addiction and usage have plummeted, and the overall cost to Portuguese society of the drug "problem" (inclusive of the spread of HIV through shared needles) has been massively reduced.

This is how Democratic Libertarianism works.

9

The Environment: Existential Security

Eighty miles north of the Arctic Circle and one thousand miles northwest of Anchorage, you will find the city (more of a village; population 370) of Kivalina, which stands on an island in the Chukchi Sea off Alaska. Home to people from the indigenous Inupiat community who have lived there since time immemorial, Kivalina is likely to be submerged forever under the Arctic's icy waters by 2025. The reason? The melting of the polar ice caps occasioned by the change in our environment.

Well to the north of Kivalina lies the joint Canadian–US North Warning System, a semicircular string of sophisticated radar systems stretching from Alaska to Iceland designed to warn of incoming Russian bombers and missiles. Many of these stations are situated on outcrops that are now in danger of becoming submerged.

The city and the radar network share one issue in common, with two (out of many) potential outcomes. The first involves the future physiological security of a population who will undoubtedly have to be moved from their homes to safer ground in Alaska. Imagine the effect if your city were suddenly ripped up and relocated. What jobs could you get? Where would the children be educated? Could you afford the housing? Everything in your life to date that stood for security would have to be relearned. It can and will be done, but at a cost.

The second involves the erosion of a key defensive system just as the adversary in question is becoming more and more bold in its incursions into American airspace and in its cyberattacks on the American political system. Here is a physiological threat of the most serious order—the inability (or reduced ability) to defend one's own borders against an enemy.

Now imagine that you put these two threats together. Imagine you are a resident of Norfolk, Virginia, and that you work at one of the country's largest naval installations, Norfolk Naval Base. Or perhaps you work at Norfolk Naval Shipyard or Naval Air Station Oceana just up the road in Virginia Beach. In the last hundred years, the sea level at Norfolk has risen by eighteen inches, about eight inches of which is attributable to the measurably rising sea level, while the other ten inches is due to the gradually sinking coastline. With the acceleration of climate change, Norfolk now outpaces the rest of the East Coast in terms of sea-level rise, with a further two-foot increase predicted in the next thirty years alone.[16] The effect of a rise that big would be devastating not only to the local population, hundreds of thousands of which would have to be relocated to new ground, but also to the defenses of this country. Physiological security at all levels would be compromised. Whether or not all of this has come about due to human dereliction, the sheer fact of the matter is that it is happening. What should be the response of government in such a situation?

In the early 1200s, there existed a city in England called Sarum. Theoretically, it was in an ideal position, perched on top of a hill near a river. Crowning the city was an enormous castle for its defense and a beautiful cathedral in which to thank God for all the population's many blessings. There was

---

16 Pat Rios, former US Navy director of facilities and environmental, mid-Atlantic region, as quoted by Public Radio International, 2016.

only one problem: For some unknown reason, the city was riddled with disease, some of it dreadful and existence-threatening, such as dysentery and the plague. There was something about that location that just did not sit well with human habitation.

The conundrum facing the city's leaders, both military and ecclesiastical, was huge. They had invested millions (by today's standards) in the castle, cathedral, and city infrastructure. Should they abandon all of that just to escape disease that mainly threatened the poor? Or should they just stick their heads in the sand and pretend it was all not happening and that everything would blow over eventually? In the end, they showed enormous courage and decided to rebuild their city, with an even better cathedral, down in the valley below them on the river. They literally tore down their city and rebuilt an even better version a couple of miles away. That city still stands today. It is called Salisbury.

Today, the whole planet is Sarum. Only the American government has decided that the ostrich approach is the more acceptable way forward, especially in the quest for short-term economic growth. The Trump administration has therefore pulled out of the Paris Agreement, appointed a climate change denier to run the EPA, and mandated that all references to climate change be expunged from EPA websites and documents. In his book *The Fifth Risk*, Michael Lewis tells of how the National Oceanic and Atmospheric Administration (NOAA), the part of the Commerce Department that monitors, tracks, and predicts our weather, was given into the hands of the CEO of AccuWeather, a man who had called for NOAA's destruction. NOAA is no longer allowed to opine on the causes or effects of climate change. Why? Because that would be an admission that climate change exists.

Yet the evidence that it does exist is all around us. From average annual temperatures that continue to rise to disappearing glaciers and melting ice caps, our climate is changing at a rate that actually is exceeding scientists' worst predictions. Not only that, but the effects of our lifestyle are increasingly being seen in disturbing phenomena, such as the mountains of plastic wandering our seas. Each year, we deposit between five million and fourteen million tons of plastic into the ocean.[17] As it breaks down, it becomes microplastic and is ingested by fish, which are then eaten by us. So far, scientists have found microplastics in 114 species of fish, half of which are consumed by humans. The problem here is not only are we ourselves ingesting this stuff but so are baby fish, which often die as a result. This results in a decrease in fish stocks overall—since the 1970s, the world's stock of fish has declined by half, some of which is due to the pollution of the seas. Some scientists now predict that the oceans could be empty of fish by 2050 due to the combination of this type of pollution, warming seas, and overfishing.

Fish are some of the healthiest foods that human beings can consume, and they are in existential danger. Beef is one of the least healthy foods that we eat, and yet its production is at all-time highs. And cows are one of the biggest contributors to greenhouse gas[18]—every year the approximately 1.4 billion cows on this planet (along with sheep, pigs, and other animals) burp into the atmosphere 14.5 percent of our greenhouse gas emissions. The culprit? Methane. Just like coal and oil, methane is highly useful to humans as an energy source but incredibly destructive to the atmosphere. And while the oil and gas industry is responsible for about a third of our methane emissions, agriculture is another primary culprit. But it is not the only one—landfills also contribute, as do decomposing plastics in seawater.[19] So the story comes full circle. But wait! There is one more aspect to the methane story, one that should keep all of us who believe in science awake into the wee hours. As the Arctic permafrost melts due to increasing global temperatures, it releases from deep below huge bubbles

---

17 "Planet or Plastic?" *National Geographic*, June 2018.

18 The Environmental Defense Fund, 2018.

19 Sarah-Jeanne Royer, University of Hawaii at Manoa, August 2018.

of methane—enough for one gigaton to enter the atmosphere by the end of the century. That will have a significant effect on temperatures, and so the cycle will continue.

Some might argue that while the level of methane emissions may not be in question, it is after all a naturally occurring phenomenon on this earth, and why are scientists making such a fuss about it? The fact is, while carbon dioxide is more prevalent in the atmosphere (due to coal and oil burning), the negative effect of methane on the environment is twenty-three times higher and traps eighty-four times more heat. Methane should therefore be the number one worry for us as we work out how to combat climate change.

The urgency inherent in that battle is enormous. The planet has already entered into what is called the "sixth mass extinction." The earth has been through five mass extinctions of its species before, the most notable being that which killed off the dinosaurs after a massive meteor strike sixty-six million years ago. Today, mainly as a result of human activity, the rate of extinction, both in plants and animals, is 100 to 1,000 times the norm and is expected to result in the disappearance of one million species.[20] Entire types of animal, plant, and ocean environments, such as coral reefs, are dying. The effect on biodiversity, on which the planet thrives, will be devastating.

As the planet disintegrates around us, however, that may not even be the main story in the media of the future. The most palpable manifestation of all this may well be planet-wide war as the world's population competes for its most precious resource—water. In 2018, Cape Town, South Africa, came within days of running out of water completely. There was even talk of towing an iceberg from Antarctica to cope with the crisis. It would have been the first time a prominent world city had completely run out of water. In June 2019, Chennai, India, achieved that dubious distinction.

The harsh realities here are that climate change is altering the geographic availability of water and that the world's population is putting more pressure

---

20   Global Assessment Report on Biodiversity and Ecosystem Services, IPBES, 2019.

on water resources as they exist today. According to a recent study by the European Commission's Joint Research Centre, the areas most at risk for conflict as a result of these twin trends are those that share significant water resources.[21] The most prominent of these are the Nile (Egypt and Sudan), the Ganges-Brahmaputra (India and Bangladesh), the Indus (India and Pakistan), the Tigris-Euphrates (Turkey, Syria, and Iraq), and the Colorado (USA and Mexico) rivers. Note that two of these (Indus and Tigris-Euphrates) are already conflict powder kegs, and two involve nations with nuclear weapons (Indus and Colorado). The researchers running the study put the chance of a major water conflict in the next fifty to one hundred years at 75 percent to 95 percent.

In North America, of course, there is another great water source that is shared across boundaries: the Great Lakes, spanning the USA and Canada. As the southern and western states in America dry out and become hotter and hotter, it is not inconceivable that the USA will start to eye Canadian water resources with increasing interest. A war with Canada? Today it seems inconceivable, but in the near future perhaps not so much so.

Polluted air, rising sea levels, depleted fish stocks, a mass extinction of species, agriculture as a major source of warming gases, and water wars. It is a bleak picture and by no means the whole one. Add to this a government, political party, and swath of the population who just do not want to believe all of this (and indeed are working in the opposite direction) and you have the makings of an existential disaster. In refusing to deal with it, our current political elite are betraying one of the most fundamental requirements of physiological security—a clean and safe environment. Yet it isn't as if something can't be done. It can, and there are plenty of examples in both science and government where we can see it being done.

The first thing to recognize is that this is indeed a human-made crisis. The Industrial Revolution, which began in Britain in the 1830s, is by no

---

21   "Global Hotspots for Potential Water Disputes." EU Science Hub, October 2018.

means over, sweeping over the planet from economy to economy. There is no doubt that, as it has done so, creating thriving middle classes in China, India, and elsewhere, it has indeed revolutionized the way in which vast populations across the world live. Poverty levels have dropped dramatically, and more people than ever before can live in relative economic security. But—and it is a huge but—we also have to recognize that the Industrial Revolution is based almost entirely on a take-and-consume model. For nearly two hundred years, we have taken what the earth has given up in terms of fossil fuels and consumed them so that more consumable products could be made and sold. That model still persists despite the advent of solar and wind energy. Indeed, it has been expanded over the years to include the voracious mining of uranium (for nuclear power and weapons), lithium (batteries of all sorts to power everything from phones to cars and some airplane systems), mercury (screens of all types), and many other toxic elements. We continue to take to make and sell—and then have real trouble in disposing of these poisonous chemicals in a safe and sustainable manner. The more we take from the planet, the more we poison the planet and the less sustainable our future becomes.

When staring this reality in the face, it is easy to become despondent and to wonder how it is that the human race can be racing toward obliteration while denying that it is doing so. Yet the truth is that there are plenty of initiatives abounding that give cause for hope. These range from new economic models to bold and persistent activism on the part of our youngest generations to breakthroughs in the science of farming. In the field of economics, let us take for a moment the example of the circular economy. This is a concept in which waste and pollution are designed out of the system, products and materials are kept in use for as long as possible (through processes such as reuse, repair, remanufacturing, and recycling), and living/biological systems are continuously regenerated. Individual aspects of the circular economy already exist and are well-known and tested. What is needed is a societal and political framework designed to bring them all together.

One example of the application of circular economy ideas lies in agriculture and initiatives to mitigate the effect on the environment of beef farming. The problem under the microscope is the production of methane. One idea for dealing with this is to produce beef (and indeed other meats) synthetically in the laboratory. The first burger so produced was consumed in 2013, and today there are numerous start-up companies getting into the business as costs fall and production can scale up. Aside from the benefit of a reduction in methane in the atmosphere, such a move would also free up a lot of farmland for other uses. Similarly, vertical farming, in which crops are grown in stacks instead of fields, achieves the same purpose. At the other end of the beef spectrum, scientists are also working on converting the bacteria in cows' stomachs from producing methane to producing much less damaging gases.

The point to all of this is that, even though we appear to stand on the brink of environmental disaster, all is not yet lost. We have the brainpower and ingenuity to grapple with the causes and reverse the damage. But it is going to take a concerted effort—and one in which government is highly proactive—to do it. The direct equivalent in history to what we need to do today can be found in JFK's extraordinary commitment in May 1961 to put a man on the moon by the end of the decade. JFK didn't do this solely for the science of it—he did it to rally the country around an objective so challenging and so mind-blowing as to unite the nation in its cause. Despite his assassination and those of his brother and Martin Luther King, not to mention the Vietnam war, the goal was achieved.

Precisely the same challenge to the nation needs to be laid down now, with the same commitment from the government to succeed. JFK was, in many ways, a Democratic Libertarian. He did not like government intervention for its own sake but he was willing to throw government weight behind major goals that pushed the nation forward or that safeguarded security (for example, the Civil Rights Act subsequently brought to fruition by LBJ). We are in the same position now. The environmental security of the nation—indeed, the entire planet—depends on the United States government coming up with a Big Hairy Audacious Goal (BHAG). A BHAG is something so big, so "out there," and so motivating that everyone will get behind it—even the skeptics. Our future and our survival are contingent upon our finding leaders willing to challenge us to meet this goal.

Ultimately, what we are talking about here is culture change, starting at the top of our nation. Not just in terms of believing in and acting on climate change, but also where our relationship as a species with nature and the world is perceived. Before widespread colonization, the aboriginal peoples of this world (including the tribes of North America, the aborigines of Australia, the Maori of New Zealand, and the Hottentots of South Africa) all had one thing in common: They revered and cared for nature. They were part of it and it of them.

"The great river flows from the mountains to the sea. I am the River, the River is me."

This saying comes from the Maori tribes of Whanganui in New Zealand and refers to the Whanganui River of the North Island. When the British colonized New Zealand in the eighteenth century, they formed a treaty with the Maoris pledging to join them in caring for and revering the environment. But the British never upheld their side of the bargain and proceeded to desecrate the Whanganui River for centuries. Until March 20, 2017, that is. On that day, an extraordinary thing happened: The New Zealand Parliament passed legislation declaring the river and its entire environs to be a legal person with "all the rights, powers, duties and liabilities" that come with that designation. (Contrast this with the US Supreme Court declaring corporations to be legal persons!) And it's not just in New Zealand that this is happening—it is spreading to countries like India and even, here in the US, Ohio, where voters recently granted legal standing to Lake Erie.

Granted, the mental and cultural shift from regarding corporations as people to doing the same for rivers, lakes, and mountains is a massive one. But the good news is that we have done it before. We can do it again. The science is there, the people are there, the ideas are there. They just need to be harnessed and given the space and resources to grow.

10

The Security Guarantee: Law and Order

Security: the state of being free from danger or threat; the state of feeling safe, stable, and free from anxiety or fear. Synonyms: safety, protection, stability, certainty, happiness, confidence. Origin: *Securus* or *Securitas*—Latin for free from care.

The second level on Maslow's hierarchy is all about security. Note that security is defined both as a "state" or a "feeling," and that it is about the "freedom" that comes from being safe. As Maslow himself realized, security is both physical and mental. It is therefore much more than just physical safety (although that is a big part of it). It also includes the provision of an environment in which a person can feel free from worry or care about their future.

As such, in a political sense security embraces both national and personal safety but *also* includes health, financial well-being, and social security. It is also arguable that, in the modern world, the ability to attain these must involve the security afforded by education.

Why, in the twenty-first century, is security so important? And why is it vital that governments—even those with a libertarian bent—be the guarantors of security? The short answer is that real security in society is something we have had for only a very short period of time, and even then, it has been a commodity that only certain parts of the world have been able to achieve. But in that time we have seen the resounding benefits in terms of economic growth, health, and personal freedom that real security brings. Despite all the terrible news we hear and see from around the world every day on our various screens, the truth is that the world is experiencing less poverty, greater health and well-being, and less fighting than at any period in human history. To lose these gains through a loss of security would usher in an era of unimaginable horror and degradation, which nobody in their right mind wants to see.

The most relevant historical equivalent to such a state can be found in the fall of the Roman Empire. Not for nothing was the state-of-being of Roman rule over Europe, the Middle East, and North Africa called Pax Romana. Although the world 2,000 years ago was indeed a violent place, Roman rule brought with it the rule of law, peace, economic growth, an increase in life expectancy, and greater health and hygiene. You have only to visit the remains of Roman towns and cities across Europe to marvel at their water and sewerage systems, for example, as well as their roads and cultural centers. When the empire finally fell to the Germanic hordes from the north, all of this disappeared, leading to what we now call the Dark Ages. Health declined, life expectancy decreased, and people actually became shorter as a result of their malnutrition. Europe once again descended into a patchwork of warring tribes, and violence ruled. It was the institutional memory of this that caused the Allies to fight so bitterly hard against the threat of Hitler and Nazism. As Churchill put it:

. . . if we fall, then the whole world, including the United States, including all that we have known and cared for, will sink into the abyss of a new Dark Age made more sinister, and perhaps more protracted, by the lights of perverted science.

Only since the Allied victory in 1945 has the world known and tasted security, even in an imperfect state. Before then, the world was a very violent place in which individual security played second fiddle to the bellicosity of those in power. Prior to the 1800s, war was a favored instrument of securing and defending power bases, whether the rulers were monarchs, tribal chiefs, or privateers and mercenaries. As an individual, you were likely to either be called upon to fight or to find your homestead caught up in the horrors of war and retribution. Indeed, such conditions were among the primary motivators of the fourth great migration from the United Kingdom to the American colonies in the 1700s—war-torn peoples from the Scottish Borders (one of the most violent places in Britain at that time) fled across the Atlantic to put down roots in the Carolinas and eventually most of what we now call the American South. What were they looking for? A measure of security—a feeling of safety. In the 1800s, the violence became more institutionalized as great empires battled it out around the world to achieve dominance. And, of course, the first half of the last century brought about the two greatest conflagrations the world has ever seen.

What we learned as a result of those terrible wars is that a confident, peaceful, prosperous society is a basic and fundamental component of world peace. It is arguable that World War II would never have happened had Britain, France, and the United States not punished Germany so severely for its transgressions in World War I. The Treaty of Versailles imposed such massive penalties on Germany that its postwar economy could not possibly cope. The aftermath of hyperinflation and grinding poverty led to resentment and the perfect opportunity for antidemocratic forces to come to the fore, promising revenge, law and order, and prosperity. Luckily for all of us, General Marshall and President Truman recognized this error when contemplating the post–World War II world and opted to rebuild their enemies rather than grind them down. In doing so, they provided security for the citizens of those nations, allowing for them not only to feel safe but also to build democratic societies in which everyone could feel physically, financially, and socially secure.

The postwar international order that the United States built in the fifty years after 1945 was nothing short of unprecedented. It established economic and financial security through the Bretton Woods Agreement. It led the way in the foundation of the United Nations, a body designed to promote not only world peace but also health and social stability. It helped found—and guaranteed—the NATO alliance. Recognizing free trade as being something that lifts all boats (in the aggregate), it pursued and encouraged trade treaties around the world and provided leadership to the major economies of the world. In the peace and security that followed, other nations were inspired to add to this framework, including the founding of the European Union (as it is now), perhaps the most singular and successful agreement ever to have taken place to secure the peace in the war-torn continent of Europe.

Nobody is claiming that this framework has been free of flaws or that there have not been problems. None of the institutions cited have been free from error, and the United States itself has made some spectacular blunders—Vietnam, Nicaragua, and Iraq among them. But, taken as a whole, the world is a better place because of the postwar American agenda. What the leaders of the country understood was that American leadership in maintaining the peace (even through the Cold War and through nuclear arms), and defending Western values acted as a guarantor of its own national security. That, in its own right, begets domestic security, which, in turn, sets up the conditions needed for individual, personal security.

This is a relationship that our current president, Donald J. Trump, clearly neither understands nor cares about. His full-scale assault on America's strongest and most loyal allies (while curiously sucking up to Vladimir Putin) threatens the very basics of the infrastructure that his predecessors so carefully built. His imposition of tariffs on the European Union, Canada, Japan, and Mexico has outraged and alienated nations who naturally align with the United States on maintaining world peace and economic security. His withdrawal from both the Paris Agreement on the environment and the Iran nuclear deal undermine them and call into question whether the word of the United States can ever be trusted again. In doing all of this, Trump is playing to his base, all the time ignoring the fact that, if he weakens the basis for world security, he weakens national security and therefore that of the very people he is playing to. This is how extreme versions of the Authoritarian Right work—divide and conquer, play to the fears of your base, and ignore the wider consequences of your actions. It is a direct result of a wannabe dictator's need to narrow his selectorate—in this case the rust belt working class who have placed their trust in him to restore to them their factories and their previous ways of life. Interestingly, however, he might just be alienating the other really important part of his winning coalition—business leaders. Tariffs rarely work well for large multinational corporations, and the leaders of these firms are becoming increasingly nervous about the direction that Trump is taking.

In a Democratic Libertarian world, based on wide selectorates and the desire to provide security at all levels of Maslow's hierarchy, a cohesive world peace led by a strong America is recognized as the foundation for peace at home and the ability to achieve security across the societal spectrum. That does not mean that defense spending needs to remain at its present levels, however. And Democratic Libertarians can agree with Trump that NATO partners need to contribute more to the communal defense pot. But that can only happen in an atmosphere of mutual trust and interdependence. It is quite possible to imagine a world in which this responsibility is shared more equitably and where the United States can reduce the share of its budget taken up by defense without the infrastructure of world security being fatally undermined.

In a world that is broadly at peace, a nation that leads in maintaining that peace—in this case, the United States—can then look internally to also maintaining a secure environment for the citizens within its borders. In a Maslovian world, it is every citizen's right to live in peace without fear of physical attack or crime under the protection of the law and the Constitution.

Ironically, this is something with which the United States has struggled since its inception and which has led to bloodshed on an unimaginable scale up until the present day. Despite the fact that the British (and others) had carved the colonies out of land that was previously home to others (what Canada now calls the First Nations), the Founding Fathers started out with intentions for their new country that were firmly based on ideas of equality and fairness under the law. Let's for a moment put aside the fact that such equality did not include women, indigenous Americans, or indentured servants. One could make a reasonable case that this was more a product of the mores of the times rather than any deliberate attempt to qualify what "equality" meant. What the authors of the Constitution—and especially James Madison and his mentor George Mason, the progenitors of the Bill of Rights—had in mind was a radical framework of human rights, protected under law, that took some of the basic principles of the Magna Carta and the English Bill of Rights to a whole new level. This would be the first written constitution in the world, conceived from the ground up, that enshrined the right of the people to live in a society that protected them, ensured that government could not suppress them, and allowed them to live in absence of fear.

But there was one issue where a historic compromise to these founding principles was made. If all thirteen colonies were to join in this epic venture that had been won with the blood of Americans, then somehow the Constitution would have to deal with an issue that some saw as one of basic morality and others one of economics: slavery. For the Southern states, preservation of the slave economy was paramount and had to be written into the Constitution—even if in ambiguous language—if they were to join this venture. Hence, for example, Article IV, Section 2, which provided for the return of any "Person held to Service or Labor" in one state "escaping into another" to be returned to their rightful owners.

The Founding Fathers struggled when they were confronted with the reality of slavery and decided to sidestep the issue by declaring that "other persons"—"other" as in not free persons or indentured servants or Indians—should be counted as three-fifths of a person when accounting for congressional representation and direct taxation. Interestingly, the sidestepping here did not allow for slaves being property and did count them as human beings, even if only 60 percent human beings. The whole issue of slavery was front and center in the framing of the Constitution, given that the entire document was designed to enable all the erstwhile colonies—both South and North—to join together in a Union. Not until the Fourteenth Amendment would African-Americans, held under slavery, be accorded (in theory) the same rights as other citizens—to live in peace under equal protection of the Constitution. I say "in theory" because under Jim Crow, the Southern system of segregation that followed the failure of Reconstruction, blacks still did not have this right. Many would argue that, even after the Civil Rights Act and the Voting Rights Act of the 1960s and the entire civil rights movement led by Martin Luther King and others, blacks are still fighting to be treated as equals in modern America. Nowhere is this more evident than in the application of the law.

In a Democratic Libertarian society, the primary duties of government rest in the provision of security to all its citizens, regardless of who they are. To repeat, at its most basic, this is the right of the citizen to live in peace under the *protection* of the Constitution. The contract here is that I, the citizen, will live under this protection and will, in return, obey legislation that is lawfully passed under the Constitution. The institutions that exist to regulate and implement these laws serve both society as a whole and individual citizens whom they are designed to protect. Thus there are laws against murder, robbery, corruption, theft, and many other acts against the individual and the state. Note, here, that the institutions designed to implement these laws are there to "serve," not to rule. The same applies to all other functions of the state. Whether we are talking about your local DMV, your state legislator, or your county sheriff, they exist to *serve* you, the citizen, and uphold the Constitution. They do not exist to rule, impose on, or strike fear into you. Remember, security is about the absence of fear. They do not exist to favor one citizen over another or one class of citizen over another.

The sayings "nobody is above the law" and "everyone is equal under the law" are the embodiment of democracy and were born in the United States of a rejection of the divine right of monarchy. This implies that the ultimate power rests with the citizenry as a whole (the nominal selectorate), although in reality it rests with the real selectorate—those who actually participate in the electoral process. But wherever it rests, it does not imply the right of one subset of the citizenry to function under a set of laws that are different from those that apply to all. This is a lesson the Trump administration appears not to have learned but is at the heart of American democracy.

From a Democratic Libertarian point of view, ultimate power resting with the people further implies that government officers are not in a position of authority over the citizenry. We, the public, do not owe any government official deference because of their position—something that many in governmental bureaucracy seem to have forgotten. Contrary to the received wisdom in an Authoritarian Right society, a policeman does not have "authority" over you. He or she is there to serve you and protect you. At times, a police officer may require that you follow instructions in order to keep the peace in a certain situation, but the phraseology here is actually very important: *keep the peace*—that is, preserve the security and absence of fear that is your right under the Constitution. This may seem overly idealistic, but the truth is that it happens every day all over these United States. Witness a parking judge who is now one of the most famous in the United States (thanks to social media), Frank Caprio, who encapsulated this idea wonderfully when he said, "I don't wear a badge under my robe. I wear a heart under my robe." He not only adjudicates the cases that come before him, he serves both society and the accused, taking into account the totality of their lives, not just the offenses with which they have been charged. Or consider the police officer who caught a young mom shoplifting food. After seeing her completely empty pantry, he went out and bought her and her children a week's supply of groceries. In a news world where we usually only hear the worst stories, these tales of service to individuals and the community by those in positions of nominal authority are legion. And so they should be, for they form the fabric of society.

And yet despite this, America is a country that lives with the presence of fear more than any other civilized nation in the world. The likelihood of being murdered in the United States, while lower than it has been for years, is still five to ten times higher than it is in Europe, Australasia, most of Asia, and all of Scandinavia.[22] It is not unusual in American families for people to have known close relatives or friends that have met their end in this way—in our own family, there are two! In our local newspapers, news of deaths by gun violence is a daily occurrence, usually meriting a couple of column inches on page six. In Europe, such news is national front page. Our police—however much they want to serve their communities—go to work every day not knowing the violence that will be coming their way. How and why does this dichotomy exist in the Western world's most idealistic nation?

The answer lies primarily in an ideology that has been taken to extremes and that has wrapped itself in the flag. That ideology is the inalienable right of citizens to be armed—without restriction—under a supposed literal reading of the Second Amendment. To the modern eye, this is one of the most vague and convoluted pieces of English writing ever to exist, which means it is wonderfully susceptible to varying interpretations that people can then swear blind is the inalienable truth. Here it is in all its glory:

---

22   United Nations Office on Drugs and Crime, 2017.

A well-regulated Militia, being necessary to the security of a free state, the right of the people to keep and bear Arms, shall not be infringed.

The NRA concentrates very heavily on the second half of the statement: the right of the people to keep and bear arms shall not be infringed. This is an absolute right of all the people, it does not specify what kinds of arms, and it shall not be infringed in any way, even through restrictions on who can buy and what they can buy. It is from that last phrase that the NRA pushes vociferously for open carry laws and regulations permitting firearms to be carried onto campuses and into bars.

The Left concentrates more on the first phrase: a well-regulated militia. The Bill of Rights, they argue, was written in an entirely different era when there was no standing army, no National Guard, and precious few police forces. Militias—groups of citizens who banded together to protect their communities—were therefore very necessary and needed to be armed. But the situation is entirely different today, and indeed we view militias pretty dimly, generally characterizing them as bands of deranged conspiracy theorists and white supremacists. There is absolutely no need for the public to be armed, and the Second Amendment is a curious relic of the past. In addition, progressives will point to the fact that the Founding Fathers could not possibly have imagined a world in which guns could fire massive amounts of bullets in just a few seconds all by themselves.

Libertarians of varying shapes and sizes, from the mainstream to the militia member, emphasize the middle of the amendment: being necessary to the security of a free state. After all, when the Bill of Rights was written, Americans had just freed themselves through armed insurrection from an autocratic and capricious monarch (or, at least, that was the general perception). Who was to say that government would always govern for the good of the people? If an equally capricious dictator appeared on the horizon, would it not be the right of the American people to use arms once again to regain their freedom? Which raises the interesting question: Does the Constitution therefore condone insurrection in the event of a current or future president arrogating to him- or herself the powers of a monarch?

Seen through these different lenses, the Second Amendment can be read in three different ways. However, it is arguable that its real relevance to society today can perhaps be better understood by going back to the Constitution and reading it in its entirety, not just in the context of this particular clause. The Bill of Rights as a whole is actually a wonderful rendering into law of Democratic Libertarianism, providing a framework in which Maslow's needs can be met and government by, of, and for the people brought into being. It guarantees freedom of speech, freedom of worship, freedom of assembly, protection against unreasonable search, the right to trial by jury, and numerous other rights that, in the words of the Fourth Amendment, secured the "right of the people to be secure in their persons, houses, papers, and effects." Or, in other words, the right to live in the absence of fear. Given that this is the driving force behind the Bill of Rights, it becomes distinctly arguable that some regulation and restriction on the right to bear arms is actually necessary to perpetuate freedom from fear, which is the very opposite of what we have today.

This can be seen in one of its bleakest of forms by the fact that law enforcement itself uses fear as a major argument for militarizing itself and for use of force. Police officers today have a right to feel fearful for their lives. It is this sad fact that has led to an environment in which police officers kill more than 1,000 people a year. In almost all cases, one of the reasons they give for these shootings is that they felt threatened. By contrast, in 2016, British police not only killed no one but actually deployed their guns a grand total of six times. How can two of the most civilized nations on earth be so different when it comes to protecting life and liberty? There is not a shadow of doubt that the life of an American policeman is much more dangerous than that of his British counterpart. However, the problems they face are very similar. Both are confronted by the perennial problem of gangs engaged in drug dealing, prostitution, human trafficking, and money laundering. Both encounter potentially dangerous situations involving domestic abuse. Both have to deal with robbers and murderers (although in the UK on a much smaller scale). So why is the American policeman faced with exponentially more danger? The answer is one word: guns.

There are now more guns in circulation in the United States than there are people. The country is awash in them—and not just handguns but semi-automatic and automatic rifles designed for mass slaughter. It is easy to get a gun despite systems of background checks nominally designed to keep them out of the hands of the wrong people, such as criminals and the mentally ill. And so it is that, in the first five months of 2018, there were *twenty-two* mass shootings in public schools in the United States. The last such incident in the United Kingdom was in 1996. So it is that a deranged gunman could slaughter hundreds of concert goers in Las Vegas while barricaded on the balcony of his hotel room. It's not that atrocities don't happen elsewhere in the Western world—they do. Paris has seen a series of attacks in the last few years by ISIS extremists. A bomber in Manchester, England, was able to kill twenty-three people and wound another 139. But these were political attacks, motivated by religious ideology. What sets the United States apart is such incidents are far more frequent and, for the most part, not related to politics or religious ideology.

How is it that more than 30,000 people a year are killed by guns in America? And why do mass shootings happen with such frequency and regularity? How is it that children cannot go to school without fearing that perhaps today will be the day when their school is targeted? Do they not have the same right as the rest of us to live a life free from fear? Should black males live in fear of being gunned down by nervous police? And should the police themselves have to live in fear because every traffic stop could involve someone with a gun? The response of the Authoritarian Right in these circumstances is to arm up even further those who have a responsibility to protect. Thus we have police departments that resemble small armies and have the feel of an occupying force rather than your local friendly copper who is there to protect and serve you. Thus we have the plainly idiotic suggestion that teachers should be armed in the schools in which they teach. The response is always that the only way to counter a baddie with a gun is to be armed yourself. And that is the product of an ideology that says that it is the absolute sacred right of the average American to be armed to the teeth with whatever weapon he or she deems appropriate to securing their safety without restriction or regulation. How sad it is that the basic right of the citizenry to live in the absence of fear, guaranteed by the government, is given over to the barrel of a gun wielded by the citizens themselves.

It was not always like this. While today the National Rifle Association is closely associated with vociferous lobbying of mainly conservative politicians to abort any attempts to restrict or regulate gun ownership, the association back in the 1930s was very much in favor of such restrictions and regulations. Karl Frederick, the NRA president in 1934, testified as such to Congress as they considered the first federal gun control law, the National Firearms Act. Frederick's testimony would have been utter heresy today:

"I have never believed in the general practice of carrying weapons. I seldom carry one. . . . I do not believe in the general promiscuous toting of guns. I think it should be sharply restricted and only under licenses."[23]

This approach by the NRA to the issue of regulation persisted all the way into the late sixties, when it supported the Gun Control Act of 1968. Only after that, with the advent of new, politically motivated leadership, did the organization turn into the lobbying machine it is today. The NRA's stance, ideologically based in the Second Amendment, is essentially that

---

23   Congressional Record.

there should be no restrictions on gun ownership and no regulation. That is libertarianism run amok and is grounded in a belief that the Second Amendment allows everybody to carry guns just in case the federal government becomes evil and tries to take their rights away. What is brilliant is that these gun libertarians have convinced the Authoritarian Right to adopt their cause and have made it a litmus test for their continued political survival. It's not necessarily that conservatives really believe this stuff—it's just that they love the money they get and are fearful of losing their seats. In making this pact with the gun lobby and the firearms industry that it increasingly represents, Republican politicians (and a few Democrats) are essentially content to endanger the security of both society and the individual by promoting an entirely false argument that individual security is enhanced by gun ownership. Ironically, study after study has shown that increased household gun ownership is highly correlated with increases in both homicide and suicide.[24] So much for increased individual security.

In a Democratic Libertarian America, ownership of guns would still be allowed to the general population, but there would be an insistence on reducing the potential harm to others. Remember that the essence of the second Maslovian tier in the pyramid—and of Democratic Libertarianism—is the right to live in an absence of fear. That applies to every single individual in society, inclusive of the police. If we are to reduce the fear in America today and relieve the stress on police forces (as well as teachers, health workers, schoolchildren, and the average man or woman on the street), then we have to regulate gun ownership and provide the framework for gun owners to enjoy their right in a way that is safe and not harmful to others. After all, we do this with cars, motorbikes, alcohol, aircraft, knives, poisons, and any number of other potential dangers to individuals and society. It is beyond ironic that the Authoritarian Right wants to crack down so hard on drugs (from marijuana on up) and yet refuses to do the same thing with guns. But,

---

24   American Public Health Association; Harvard School of Public Health, 2018.

in saying this, we have to be conscious that we are starting from a point that is almost beyond control. It's like the old Irish joke where a man comes across a fork in the road and asks an old-timer standing there which fork he should take. "Well," responds the old-timer, "if I were you, I would not start from here." Sadly, though, "here" is exactly where we do need to start.

First, we need to get the principles straight. The Second Amendment exists. Unless we want to go down the road of trying to pass a constitutional amendment to obviate or change this (very likely a bloody, long, and divisive road), then we just have to accept that. Similarly, there would seem to me to be little point in perpetuating the argument of what it means. While you can argue all day long that "a well-armed militia" does not mean every Tom, Dick, or Harry in the United States, the Supreme Court of this country has recently ruled that the interpretation should be that individuals should have the right to own guns. So, let's start from there. Yes, it is your right to own and carry a gun. But does that mean any gun?

In the time of the Founding Fathers, a gun was a musket, requiring reloading every time it was fired. It most certainly was not an automatic or semiautomatic weapon, capable of killing tens and wounding hundreds of people in a matter of seconds. Can we therefore define what types of guns people may legally own? In 1994, Congress passed the Federal Assault Weapons Ban as part of a much wider bill relating to violent crime. This proscribed the manufacture for civilian use of semiautomatic "assault weapons" and associated ammunition for a ten-year period. Unfortunately, in what was one of his weakest moments as president, George W. Bush allowed this "sunset clause" to go by without attempting to renew the ban. Since then, the NRA has used this to argue that no weapons can or should be so regulated under the Second Amendment. Taking this argument to its most absurd conclusions (*reductio ad absurdum*, as the Romans would have said), the NRA would have you able to buy pretty much anything that fires bullets or missiles from a weapon designed to do so. But that is not what the Second Amendment says, nor does it preclude the regulation of arms ownership, as all court rulings affirmed in cases seeking to overturn the Assault Weapons Ban. There is absolutely nothing in the Constitution that prevents us from building a regulatory structure around gun ownership to keep it safe.

With this in mind, we can look for inspiration to other countries where gun ownership is legal but regulated. In 1996, Australia saw a gun-related massacre of thirty-five people in the Tasmanian town of Port Arthur. There had been eleven similar attacks in the decade before that. The conservative (let me repeat that—conservative) government of Australia responded by introducing strict regulations surrounding gun ownership, including an outright ban on automatic and semiautomatic weapons as well as licensing laws that involved background checks and waiting periods for other types of firearms. They also launched a buy-back program that saw 650,000 weapons handed in to authorities. Since then, there has been no mass shooting of the type seen in Port Arthur, and the rate of gun homicides has fallen to 0.13 deaths per 100,000 people (the equivalent in the United States is 3.0 per 100,000). Notable here is that guns are not illegal in Australia (more than three million are in circulation)—they are just well regulated.

Similarly, in Canada, the rate of gun homicides is 0.5 per 100,000, even though the incidence of gun ownership is actually very high—nearly 25 per 100 people. This too is due to strict regulation, including a sixty-day waiting period to buy a gun, a ban on assault rifles, and stringent background checks on people's criminal, mental, and addiction profiles.

In the United Kingdom, after the Dunblane school shooting to death of seventeen people in 1996, a series of regulations were enacted that ensured that such a massacre has not happened since. These included a ban on assault rifles and other types of guns as well as the need to register as a gun owner and specify why the gun is needed. Britain has 0.7 gun homicides per 100,000 people and one of the lowest gun-ownership profiles in the world.

Gun rights advocates in the United States often point to Switzerland as a place where the right to gun ownership is also enshrined into law, as indeed it is. Swiss ownership of firearms (excluding those issued to citizens as part of the membership of state-sanctioned militias—the equivalent of the Swiss army) equates to about 24 guns per 100 residents, which is low compared to the United States but high compared to other Western nations. However, even here, the acquisition of both guns and ammunition is tightly controlled and requires, among other things, the provision of a valid passport, a clean up-to-date criminal record, and a residential address. Automatic (but not semiautomatic) weapons are banned, and public carrying of weapons is heavily restricted. In other words, gun ownership is legal but controlled.

In each of these countries, it is not illegal to own a gun. Indeed, in some of them, gun ownership is relatively high. Yet, in all of them, gun violence is suppressed by regulation that is well thought through, fair, and designed to ensure that guns are owned by people who are qualified (and, more import-ant, not *dis*qualified) to own and use them. We do exactly the same for cars, private planes, knives, heavy machinery, and any number of other things. Why on earth can the same not be done for guns? Arguments to the con-trary tend to rely on both ideology and fear, neither of which are a logical basis for law. A Democratic Libertarian government, therefore, would regu-late the types of guns to be owned, who may own them, how they may be bought, and where they can be legally carried. And the basis for these laws would rest in the twin principles of respecting rights while preserving the ability of people to live in the absence of fear.

One final word on the subject of law and order: whether or not the state has the right to take the life of a person, either judicially or extrajudicially. We have already briefly examined the deaths at the hands of the police of over 1,000 people a year in the United States. For certain segments of the population—especially black males—this is a statistic that induces fear and rightfully so. But we have also seen that the police live in fear them-selves, leading to behaviors that escalate the possibility of violence. Neither of these situations should be permissible in a society that promises its cit-izens the right to live in the absence of fear. Imagine, if you will, a society in which the logical regulation of firearms reduced this fear, reduced the ability of criminals and gangs to lay their hands on weapons, and reduced the fear experienced by police. Imagine then the degree to which we could also reduce the number of lives taken by the police themselves—indeed, in which we could virtually eliminate the need for the state to assume for itself the right to take a life. That it is possible is amply demonstrated by other civilized nations who have achieved this. A nation that believes it is exceptional should be able to do the same.

But there is one other area in which the state in America assumes this same right for itself: the death penalty. The American judicial system is highly punitive, perhaps reflecting the Puritan roots of New England and the violent Scots-Irish roots of the South. Whatever the reason, the US justice system appears to be much less concerned with rehabilitation of criminals (which is the root of most judicial systems in the West) than it is with retribution. Nowhere is this more evident than in the retention of the death penalty—a system of ultimate retribution, it should be said, that has no basis in social logic other than an interpretation of the Old Testament (an eye for an eye and a tooth for a tooth). There is no evidence whatsoever in a country with a homicide rate that is far higher than its Western peers that the death penalty has any deterrent effect.

Worse, since its founding in 1992 in New York City, the Innocence Project has helped free more than twenty death row inmates who were wrongly convicted—and there are many more that have been helped by similar organizations. If society is construed to provide security, surely it cannot condone the taking of innocent lives on the basis of judicial error. So let's put this on the table right here and now: The death penalty does not guarantee personal security either to individuals or to society as a whole. It is merely a mechanism by which society can feel that it has gained a measure of revenge. It's not that we don't understand this need for revenge—especially if the victims are defenseless, such as women, children, or the elderly. We become rightfully and righteously angry and want to see "justice done." But the history of the United States in this regard has not been a glorious one, whether we are talking about judicial executions or lynchings. The death penalty just does not work as a deterrent—a fact recognized by all our Western cohorts. It is time that we followed their example, and a Democratic Libertarian society would do so.

A Physiological Manifesto

No citizen is ever to be denied their basic right to security—neither in food, health, nor the environment.

Eradication of homelessness through the thoughtful provision of low-cost housing options in all major cities

A living minimum wage

Controlled distribution (and partial legalization) of drugs

Reform of the judicial system

Maintenance of Pax Americana

Re-emphasis of the concept of Servant Leadership

Acceptance of the reality of the Second Amendment but with informed legislation and enforcement of fair gun regulation

Abolition of the death penalty

11

Society's Bedrock: Financial Security

We live in a capitalist society. Why? Because, to bastardize Churchill's famous quote about democracy, "it is the least worst option that we have." Communism and socialism have both, for the most part, been shown not to work, whereas (for all its flaws) capitalism has, over the long term, lifted all boats on a global scale. Has it done so fairly and equitably? No. Are all peoples and nations on a level playing field? No. Nonetheless, capitalism has succeeded where no other system has in lowering global poverty levels substantially.

In 1981, the World Bank estimated that 41 percent of the world was living in extreme poverty. By 2016, the same institution estimated that poverty affected "only" 9.1 percent of the world's population—a massive decline by any measure.[25] But *The Economist*, one of many publications that reported on this progress, also warned that this reduction was slowing and would become much more difficult in the future. Much of the improvement had occurred

---

25   *The Economist*, March 2017.

in Asia and South Asia, inclusive of China and India. Those lagging behind are primarily in sub-Saharan Africa, particularly in countries where dictators rule (and, therefore, who have to keep happy a very small winning coalition).

In a democratic society, capitalism has to be harnessed differently. The winning coalition is wider, which means the population as a whole needs to be kept financially secure. Why? Because ultimately, physiological security in a capitalist society depends on financial security. There are millions of Joe and Jane Electors who have to keep food on their tables, their children clothed, and roofs over their heads—and preferably, have enough to go to Disneyland once in a while, buy the latest iPhones, and, in modern society, make sure that Grandpa and Grandma are OK. Absence of fear in this instance equates to a degree of certainty. I am certain that I will be able to pay the mortgage next month, that I can keep the car on the road, and that little Joe can go to summer camp. And that certainty comes from two things: gainful employment and social security. In a modern Western society, therefore, one of the primary focuses of government, after national security and law and order, must be the financial security of all members of that society.

If a government fails to provide at least this basic framework, it risks the security of society as a whole. Sadly, failure comes in many forms:

- Lack of healthy, sustainable economic growth. Here we part ways with traditional socialists who emphasize the central ownership of production and, in some cases, question the value of growth. *Sustainable* growth is that which enables an economy to grow at a rate that does not stress its overall underpinnings but at the same time enables people to improve on their lot, build savings and assets, and pass on the building blocks for success and security to their children. Usually, when growth is not sustainable, it leads to . . .

- Booms and busts. When an economy overheats, there is what is euphemistically known on Wall Street as a "correction." Sometimes these are mild, sometimes brutal. Who can forget pictures of employees of Bear

Stearns and Lehman Brothers carrying their cardboard boxes out of their offices as their employers' businesses folded? Did we feel much sympathy for them? No! These were the same people who contributed to the "correction." The people for whom to feel sorry were those who lost their homes, whose small businesses shut up shop, and who were out on the street. A recession never induces feelings of security.

· Excessive income inequality. Between 1978 and 2014, US CEOs saw their average pay increase 1,000 percent[26] while the pay of an average worker rose by 11 percent. This means that CEOs today are paid more than 300 times as much as their average worker. I don't know what sort of miracle workers these CEOs are, but when I was one of them, my take-home pay never exceeded six times that of my average employee. And I think I was a pretty good CEO! *Nothing* can justify such income inequality within the same company. My father, an Anglican bishop, had a brass plaque fixed in front of him on the throne in his cathedral that said, "Sit a man ever so high, he always sits on his own ass." CEOs need to think about that. Because when employees see the C-suite literally getting away with murder, they become resentful and lose motivation. And that is good for no one's financial security.

· Excessive wealth inequality. We are by now all familiar with the fact that over 40 percent of the country's wealth is concentrated in the top 1 percent of the population. When people are struggling to make ends meet on two or three jobs, when large tracts of the population (especially racial minorities) have negative equity, when hard work does not lead to realization of the American Dream, the people become resentful and start "acting out" politically, socially, and economically. At its base, financial security depends on jobs—and not just the number of jobs available but their quality. And, whether we like it or not, the availability

---

26   *Fortune,* June 22, 2015.

of good jobs does, in some part, depend on government. Sure, there can be extraneous circumstances, such as the presence of oil or precious metals, but even then the degree to which the wealth that they generate is spread throughout the population through well-paying employment is almost totally dependent on the government and how corrupt it is. Just ask the citizens of Nigeria or Saudi Arabia.

In a democracy, it all comes down once again to the framework that the government lays down. That framework is made up of a number of different factors:

- Levels of taxation—is the amount of money you take home worth the effort you put in and/or are the benefits you receive from government worth the taxes you pay?

- Is part of the role of taxation to redistribute wealth from the wealthy to the less fortunate in society, whether monetarily or through the provision of services?

- The amounts of money in the economy and the speed with which it circulates—governments have the power to print money if they so wish, which can be a good thing or a bad thing depending on the circumstances. This, and the speed with which the money circulates, will determine the rate of inflation in the economy, which in itself is really subject to Goldilocks Theory: Too little inflation and falling prices can force the economy into recession. Too much and prices go out of control, eating into your buying power. Just right and you have the conditions for sustainable growth; most Western economies currently set the "just right" target at around 2 percent.

- Interest rates—these are the main lever with which the authorities can determine how fast money circulates, how much goes into savings, how much credit there is in the market, and whether businesses invest or not.

There remains some political/ideological discussion around who should control interest rates, but the fact is that the most stable economies generally delegate this function to an independent central bank, not beholden to politicians. In the United States that bank is the Federal Reserve.

· Trade policies—trade is a two-edged sword. Conducted fairly, on a level playing field, it can enrich all the nations of the world (and, indeed, has done exactly that), as countries export to others what they are uniquely good at producing and import goods where they do not excel. But it can also be used as a substitute for warfare, whereby nations punish each other for imagined ills in the trading system. When that happens, trade usually slows and so does global economic growth. This theory, which has stood the test of time, goes all the way back to 1776, when the Scottish economist Adam Smith published his seminal work *The Wealth of Nations*. What Smith was trying to show was that by trading in goods in which we excel, we increase the overall size of the pie. What he was arguing against was the prevailing idea of mercantilism, a theory that held that trade was a zero-sum game in which there were clear winners and losers. It is a pity that, after more than 240 years in which Smith's ideas have been proven correct time and time again, we now have an administration that wants to go back to 1775 and mercantilist ways.

These, then, are the four levers of power with which a government can regulate the economy and so determine the financial security (or insecurity) of its citizens: taxation, the quantity of money in the economy, interest rates, and trade policy. Sure, there are other levers too, such as rules and regulations (which usually affect specific industries), policies surrounding mergers and acquisitions, and banking regulations, but these are the Big Four.

The degree to which these four are deployed usually depends on one of two things: ideology and crisis management. Both are equally dangerous. Macroeconomics (the workings of economies at their highest level) is a relatively simple discipline. Even though it is often derided as the "dismal science," the fact is that things usually go catastrophically wrong when one of the levers is pulled in the wrong direction. In the 1920s, too much money was allowed into the economy, causing it to overheat. The reaction of government to this was disastrous, with money being cut off just at the time that it should have been pumped into the failing economy, and trade being severely restricted at the same time. This was a case of three lever motions going wrong. In the 2000s, relaxation of banking regulations under the Clinton administration led to an oversupply of bad credit into the economy, which almost brought the banking system down and, with it, some of our weaker industries, such as automotive. Today, trade levers are being pulled in exactly the wrong direction (Trump's eighteenth-century education leading him to believe this is a zero-sum game), which will, mark my words, lead to recession.

At times of crisis, however, government has proven it can use the levers to restore calm and stability. At the end of his administration, George W. Bush injected billions into the economy and instituted rules to save the banking industry. His successor, Barack Obama, carried these policies on, saving the auto industry as well. So, government does have its (very important) place in remedying economic malfunction and preventing all-out disaster.

But, I am sure you would agree, better never to have been in this situation in the first place. In a strictly libertarian world, governments would not intervene in such crises. Better to let the markets self-regulate their way out of it, and if that means widespread financial insecurity, then so be it. Indeed, government would have very little power over the economy at all, with all the possible levers at its disposal set to "don't get involved." That is *not* the case in a Democratic Libertarian world. In our world, you, the citizen, are free to manage your finances as you will, and financial services companies are free to offer you the means to do so. But here is the kicker—this has to be done within a framework that balances the security of the individual and the security of the economy (aka society as a whole). That will inevitably mean some element of regulation—for example, of mortgages and of Wall

Street. If mortgages are being granted willy-nilly to those that cannot afford them, and if Wall Street is packaging those mortgages up and then slicing and dicing them up into "financial instruments" that the ordinary intelligent human being cannot understand, then the stage is set for disaster. Human and corporate financial misery and insecurity follow. Government has to have the ability to say, "No, these practices are unacceptable. They endanger society and individuals and therefore will not be allowed."

The same thinking applies to equity (not equality) of wealth. If a system is overindulgent of capital and yet restricts the power of labor, then wealth is going to migrate toward capital. Here's one small example: In a (well-meaning?) attempt to encourage investment in this country, the proceeds from investment are taxed at a much lower rate than is ordinary income. So if a Silicon Valley venture capitalist—a person or firm that invests other people's money into new businesses—makes a big profit on a particular investment, that person or firm will be taxed only at a rate of 20 percent on the income from that investment. But a whiz kid down the road at Facebook making $700,000 a year would be taxed on her income at up to 37 percent. Similarly, the steelworker making $90,000 a year will pay a top tax rate of 24 percent while the company he works for pays 21 percent. The American tax system tends to reward capital rather than labor.

At the same time, Republican governments nationally and locally have fought hard in the last three decades to break the power of unions and their right to collective bargaining on behalf of their members. This, together with pressures from automation, a declining manufacturing sector, and the shift of the economy to services and online retailing, means that average real wages (after accounting for inflation) have remained stagnant for the last three decades. And so we come back to the average pay of a CEO rising by 1,000 percent from 1978 to 2014 while that of the average worker rose 11 percent.

Make no mistake—such inequity in wealth and income generation is not sustainable. It creates an insecure society in which resentment builds—especially among those trapped by chronic financial insecurity (blacks, rural whites)—that ultimately will destabilize the security of society itself.

This may seem blindingly obvious. After all, in a Western society, failure to provide this basic need comes with many attendant risks, not the least of which is losing power. Not for nothing did George H. W. Bush lose the election to Bill Clinton just months after reaching soaring heights of popularity for kicking Iraq out of Kuwait. Clinton's team made famous the phrase "It's the economy, stupid." But there was also another factor at play: Because the economy was slumping, a third candidate, Ross Perot, was able to emerge with his iconic bar charts and graphs showing just how he would fix the mess. The votes he garnered were enough to topple Bush and put Clinton in the White House. So, if you are a politician, you pay minute attention to the economy if you don't want to lose power. You need a selectorate that is feeling financially secure, well fed, and relatively certain about the future.

Much has been made of the various factors that lost Hillary Clinton the 2016 election. People were fed up with political dynasties; Clinton ran a lackluster, tone-deaf campaign; the emails scandal brought her down. All of these held a scintilla of truth. But the bedrock reason was that the Democrats had, for years, ignored the financial uncertainty plaguing people who were not part of their winning coalition—the white, disaffected populations of middle America who had lost hope in their financial futures. Thanks to the vagaries of the electoral college system—and Clinton blatantly ignoring states where hope was being lost—it was enough to do her in. Ironically, Donald Trump continues to hold on to his base in part because the economy that the Obama administration created has led to record low unemployment. Trump's tax reforms have not hurt either, giving businesses the incentive to invest for the future and to bring employment even to those who thought they had been abandoned.

The very simple reason why previously solid Democratic voters in economically ravaged parts of the country abandoned Clinton and went over to Trump is that the selectorate and winning coalition in a democracy need to have certainty—the absence of fear for their own economic futures. Trump promised them that certainty—or at least hope that someone would be on their side. Although memories are short, it is still only one decade since the United States narrowly avoided a full-on depression, with millions losing their homes and their jobs and millions more becoming underemployed (that is, they had jobs but they were not enough to meet their basic financial needs). Indeed, the American selectorate today is still jittery. While the economy has gone through one of the longest periods of recovery ever recorded, the fruits of that recovery have not been evenly distributed. The share of economic output going to workers in our economy has fallen from 64.5 percent in 1974 to 56.8 percent in 2017.[27] In that same period, real wage growth (after adjusting for inflation) has been a meager 10 percent—or 0.2 percent a year. At the same time, the richest 1 percent in our population own just under 40 percent of all the nation's wealth—more than the "bottom" 90 percent combined.[28] In his book *A Century of Wealth in America*, the economist Edward N. Wolff lays this out even more starkly. The top 20 percent of people in the United States own a whopping 90 percent of all the country's wealth, while the bottom 40 percent actually have *negative* net worth. In case you think this is normal, you should know that the top 1 percent of Americans own twice as much of their country's national wealth as their counterparts in the United Kingdom, France, or Canada do theirs.

Let's think about this for a moment. Four in ten households in the United States actually owe more than they own (their liabilities exceed their assets), while one in a hundred own 40 percent of the country's riches. At the same time, the safety net (there is a reason it is called a "safety" net) that we in America provide to those among us that fall on hard times is so weak and, in some cases, so punitive that we literally abandon a substantial portion of our overall population.

---

27   Brookings Institution, March 2018.
28   Federal Survey of Consumer Finances, July 2018.

In this, the Authoritarian Right has proven itself time and again to be willingly and knowingly culpable. And this culpability is in the DNA of the republic. Whether you go back to the institution of slavery in the South or to Hamilton's visions of a strong central government and banking system, the United States has tended always to favor capital over labor. In the modern era, the almost religious ideology of aversion to regulation and to the provision of universal health care and social security has meant that finance and industry have been able to flourish (a good thing) at the expense of the "common man" (a bad thing). As a result, the Authoritarian Right has acted consistently against both societal and personal security, violating Maslow's second tier of needs and laying the groundwork for political and societal upheaval. When entire segments of the population—urban blacks or rural whites, to name just two—get trapped by financial insecurity, they ultimately react in ways that destabilize (directly or indirectly) the security of society as a whole.

Sometimes these reactions are expressed in hostility to or rebellion against what are perceived to be the ruling classes. The French Revolution, for example, was triggered by massive rises in the price of bread, accompanied by bad harvests. Whether apocryphal or not, Marie Antoinette's "let them eat cake" comment served as an encapsulation of the perception that the monarchy, aristocracy, church, and burgeoning middle class just did not care what was happening to the poor. It did not help that the French debt, enlarged by support of the American revolution, had led to tax increases to try and resolve the situation. But, in the end, the spark put to the tinder was famine. In other situations, those in financial insecurity seek comfort in populist demagoguery that, if unchecked, leads on to dictatorship. Such was the case in Germany and Italy in the 1920s, Cuba in the 1950s, and Venezuela more recently. And, sometimes, it leads to those who feel so insecure turning inward in despair, indulging in crime and self-destruction in the form of drug dealing and usage, meth labs, alcoholism, and, more recently, the opioid crisis.

Obeying the laws of physics, each of these reactions to financial insecurity in turn leads to an equal and opposite reaction in its own right. Hostility and rebellion lead to the use of repressive force, which in turn leads to more violence until, in the end, one side or the other wins out by sheer brute force. It is extraordinarily rare that such situations resolve themselves peacefully, though perhaps South Africa was the exception in the twentieth century, thanks to the force of personality of two men: Nelson Mandela and Desmond Tutu. In the case of a turn to populism, what initially appears to be the response of populist politicians to the needs of the "ordinary man" becomes a climate of fear and the loss of liberty. Retreats into despair, crime, and drugs bring on a governmental response of "cracking down" on these things (think: the war on drugs), the militarization of law enforcement (and the language that goes with it), and an explosion in incarceration.

While the United States has not seen in modern times any intimation of insurrection or rebellion (although it came close in the 1970s), it has seen a turning inward, an increase in drug usage, and a militarization of law enforcement as a result. It has also seen the rise of populism with the election of Donald Trump and his increasing attempts to create an imperial presidency. The point is that in every one of these cases, the overall security of society is gravely weakened and can lead to collapse—witness Venezuela, Zimbabwe, post-Soviet Russia, Sudan, the Democratic Republic of Congo, and any number of other nations. Venezuela was once one of the most wealthy and sophisticated nations on earth, and now look at it. To think that the same thing could not happen in America is plain fanciful.

In a Democratic Libertarian society, the onus is on government to balance competing interests such that the possibility of financial insecurity is minimized. The big idea here is not a new one: It is to put in place policies, systems, and rules that prevent such insecurity from ever happening in the first place.

Since the 1980s and the advent of monetarist and "trickle-down" economics, one of the most reviled economists has been John Maynard Keynes, a British academic who changed economic thinking and governmental policies in the most fundamental way with the publication of his most important work in 1936, *The General Theory of Employment, Interest, and Money*. At the heart of his thinking was that government has the ability to modulate economic swings through intervention, thus preventing disasters that lead to financial insecurity. *The General Theory* was published in the midst of the Great Depression, which, in both the United States and Great Britain, had caused devastating hardship to over a quarter of their respective populations. What Keynes proposed was that, in times of economic downturn, governments should spend money, injecting liquidity into the economy and so engineering recovery. This was the basis of FDR's New Deal, in which huge sums of money were injected into the American economy so as to bring back employment through government programs. Whether the New Deal succeeded or not is a matter of hot debate, with some economists claiming that what really saved the US economy was World War II.

There was another part to Keynes's theory, though, which has gone all but ignored for the last seventy years. And that is, during *good years*, governments should build surpluses with which to fund spending during downturns. It's the ultimate expression of saving for a rainy day, except politicians of all hues forgot about this very important part of the theory. They spent during the bad times, but as soon as the good times returned, they insisted on reducing tax rates and giving back the surpluses to the taxpayer. While laudable from a small-government point of view, what this did was push up deficits and national debt. In the present day, this has been taken even further, with taxes being reduced in the midst of a robust and lengthy recovery, ballooning the debt and providing a stimulus to the economy it did not need.

Where government should be planning for the bad times, it has often hastened on or exacerbated those bad times by ridiculous (or at least ill-thought-out) economic policies. Whether this was Hoover refusing to inject money into the economy at the beginning of the Great Depression, or Clinton deregulating the banks, or Trump pushing through a major tax break in the midst of a strong economy, government has proven itself adept at making the wrong decision at the wrong time.

While I am not in the business of pushing Keynesian theory (although I believe it is still more convincing than the trickle-down economics beloved of the Right), I am making the argument that government is duty-bound to provide a framework that enables growth while at the same time minimizing the possibility of endemic financial insecurity. The 2008 meltdown of the financial and housing markets was a function not only of the capitalist system but also of very poor government decisions in the Clinton era, when banking was deregulated and allowed to indulge in self-serving practices that ultimately brought the system crashing down. When government favors the financial sector or capital above all else (i.e., when it sees this as being the basis of its winning coalition), it creates an environment in which a tiny proportion of the population is able to enrich itself at the expense (in this case, the catastrophic expense) of the population at large. That creates massive financial insecurity that, in turn, makes society as a whole that much more insecure and more vulnerable to manipulation by unscrupulous populist politicians. It also means that governments have to involve themselves in curing the problem (in 2008, through the banking bailout, the insurance bailout, and the automotive bailout). However necessary these things are to prevent total meltdown, they infuriate the Left and many in the population because they look as if government is actually siding with the very people who caused the problem in the first place. Trust in the political system erodes even further, enabling the populist manipulator to wreak his havoc even if he himself comes from that very same gilded class.

It would be better to have systems in place that prevent such a situation from ever arising in the first place. In this both the Authoritarian and Libertarian Right are conflicted and confused. On the one hand, there are those who insist on rigid balanced budgets, and on the other, those who insist on returning surpluses (even when there aren't any) to taxpayers. In some states, there are also movements to cap tax rates by legislation or constitutional amendment. All of these are supposedly designed to rein in government and its supposed tendency to spend way beyond its limits, but all of them are extraordinarily bad policy from the point of view of financial security. For, in the event of an economic catastrophe (see 2008) or even a downturn, the role of government should be to preserve security. Sometimes that means spending to resuscitate the economy or even bailing out sectors that are deemed critical to economic survival. Government has to have the flexibility to do this but at the same time squirrel away money in the good times. Ironically, the only time in recent history in which the federal government has been in surplus was at the end of the Clinton administration. George W. Bush's immediate reaction upon coming to power was to return this surplus to the taxpayer through cuts. Given the abject state of the economy at the end of his tenure, he might have wished he had saved up those surpluses.

Whereas the Libertarian Right strongly desires balanced-budget laws and the removal of government from people's lives, the premise of a *Democratic* Libertarian is to minimize government involvement in people's lives within the context of assuring societal and individual security. If you don't have a job, have lost your home, and can't feed your kids, you are much less likely to be someone who can uplift society as a whole. As such, there needs to be a framework in which the individual retains as much control as he or she can over their finances, while being protected by laws that minimize the possibility of their being damaged either by the unscrupulous and the greedy or by the economic system spiraling out of control. I would suggest that such a framework would include some or all of the following:

- *A very simple income tax system* in which capital and labor are treated the same and in which there are just three tax bands and no deductions at all

- *The use of taxes to build equity in society* through the provision of services and safeguards to the less fortunate

- *Legislation or a constitutional amendment that requires balancing of aggregate budgets over a specified period*—let's say twenty years, for the sake of argument

- *A reduction in the reliance on sales taxes as a means to raise revenue*
- *A simplified and segregated banking system* in which banks are not allowed to trade on their own accounts or to slice and dice loans into securities; this would include mortgages
- *Continuation of the FDIC*
- *Continued severe prosecution of financial crimes and corruption*

The first of these is one of the most important. Over many decades, tax laws have become a primary instrument of social and economic legislation that otherwise would not have been possible, inclusive of massive amounts of pork and the ability to redistribute wealth, usually in favor of capital. As such, the number of vested interests represented by the current tax code numbers in the thousands. Here are a couple of the ways tax law has been used to direct social and economic interests:

- To increase the overall level of home ownership. Once viewed as one of the ways in which to increase wealth overall in the economy, it was believed that a property-owning population would be a wealthier population that would sustain a growing economy. And so deduction of mortgage interest from taxes became one of the most popular tweaks to the tax code ever. Except that it did not quite work out that way, as banks lent to ever-riskier prospects to keep mortgage lending growing and so triggered the massive housing crash of 2008. My wife and I, who were living in Phoenix (one of the epicenters of the crash), saw it from the inside. Our house, which we had bought for $410,000 in 2001, was worth $750,000 by 2006. When we sold it in 2010, we got $300,000 for it. The mortgage interest deduction did indeed push up home ownership, but it also induced behaviors, in both banking and the population as a whole, that brought about horrific financial insecurity. In this area, government perhaps should have just not been involved at all.

· Differential tax rates for income and capital gains. The idea here was to
boost investment in business (especially new businesses) by taxing capital
gains at a much lower rate than wage income. So, if you are an investment banker or a venture capitalist and you win big on an investment,
you pay a much lower proportion of your income from the deal than
does Joe Shmoe from his wage income. The policy may have boosted
investment for a while, but its overall effect was to redistribute wealth
from wage earners to capital investors, widening the wealth gap and creating an atmosphere of financial insecurity. Today, with venture investments at a historic low and businesses unwilling to invest their large cash
piles (instead paying greater dividends to their investors and buying back
their own shares), the policy has been turned on its head, and investment
is slowing while the wealth redistribution has accelerated.

These are just two examples where tax policy has been used to promote
major policy on a nationwide basis. But there are thousands of others that have
been used to promote specific industries—oil or soybeans, for example—or
even specific companies within certain legislative constituencies. Not only is
this an inefficient way of making and implementing policy, it is one that is
ripe for the proliferation of corruption and has invariably led to lack of transparency and the accumulation of wealth in corners of the economy that do
not actually need government help. In other words, government is not only
spending its own money unwisely, it is failing to garner income from where it
should, adding to our deficit and increasing overall financial insecurity.

What I am suggesting is a complete rewrite of the tax code down to a few
essential basics that would tax all at the same few levels—say, 5 percent, 15 percent, and 25 percent at certain income thresholds—without deductions, and
would prohibit the use of taxation legislation from being the vehicle for any
other type of policy maneuvering. You want to promote home ownership?
Then legislate for that in a separate bill. You want to promote solar energy?
Same applies. Once again, "you will say I am a dreamer." Once again, I will

say "I am not the only one." While there will undoubtedly be wailing and gnashing of teeth—especially from the lobbyists—a Democratic Libertarian Congress and president could indeed pass such reform. And the winners would be the wider selectorate, the people who depend on wage income, the people who would not have to spend money on filling in huge, opaque tax returns (sorry, H&R Block and Intuit), the people who would keep more of their income while those further up the scale paid their fair shares.

At the same time, states and major cities that levy income taxes would be urged to follow the same path of simple, striated tax bands with no exemptions or deductions. They would also be encouraged to reduce their reliance on sales taxes, the most regressive type of tax that exists. By levying the same rate of tax on goods purchased by all, regardless of their wealth, sales taxes penalize the poor far more than they do the rich or even the middle class. Such taxes reduce purchasing power for the poor and make it more difficult for them to earn their way out of the poverty trap. A system that operates solely in a simple income tax code, payable above an agreed level of income, is more equitable and allows more mobility at the bottom end of the wealth scale.

Of course, some states are proud that they have no income or sales taxes, relying on taxation of property as their primary source of income. Arguably, this is actually unfair on the wealthy and on property owners, but it is the intricate linkage of property tax to education that is much more worrisome—and this we will deal with later in this book.

All this being said, no country can survive forever if it is piling up debt to pay for its government. Going back to Keynes, a government should have the ability to pump money into the economy during bad times but also should save money (run surpluses) in the good times. Strict libertarian (or neo-libertarian) ideas of requiring annual balanced budgets, whether nationally or at the state level, strip government of this flexibility and therefore of its ability to provide financial security for society as a whole. Similar ideas of capping taxes at arbitrary levels (whether monetary or as a proportion of GDP) are equally as idiotic from the same perspective. If government is not able to raise taxes when it needs to in order to provide both financial and social security, then you take away one of its primary roles and condemn those at the bottom of the pile to abject misery every time a recession comes around.

But—and it is a big but—this does not mean that government should not operate within broader constraints where taxation, spending, and deficits are concerned. There was a time when Republicans were vocally worried about deficit spending and the level of national debt. Over the last forty years, that worry seems to have gone out the window.

US Government Debt, 1790–2015

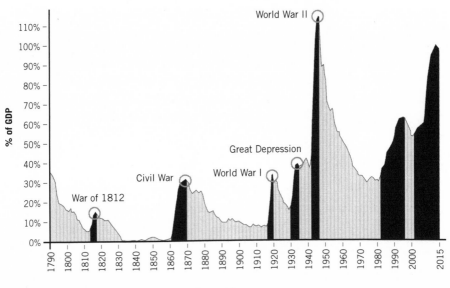

Source: Metrocosm

When Reagan came to power in 1980, the national debt stood at 32 percent of GDP, a level that had been broadly maintained since 1973. Prior to that, governments had fought to bring down the debt from its all-time high of 119 percent of GDP at the end of World War II.[29] Reagan famously lowered taxes during a boom economy (when, according to Keynes at least, he should have been running surpluses); Bush 41 then had to fight Iraq in Desert Storm, after which the economy sank into recession (the two events were not connected); Clinton fought to balance the budget and ended up with a surplus, halting the inexorable increase in the debt ratio, which now stood at 62 percent; Bush 43 then embarked on a ruinous war that cost trillions of dollars (which he managed to keep out of budget calculations for years) and then was hit by the simultaneous crashes in the housing market and on Wall Street. By the time Obama came to power, huge amounts of deficit spending, including a $400 billion stimulus package, had started to push the ratio above 80 percent and on to 105 percent by the time he left power. But, with a solid recovery under way it is arguable that this could have been reined in after 2016 had President Trump and the Republicans not signed into law a $1 trillion tax cut, which the Office of Management and Budget calculates will push the ratio up to 108 percent in 2019—the highest since World War II.

We used to mock the likes of Italy, Greece, and Spain for similar ratios, assuring ourselves that we were much cleverer than they were. It turns out we are not. Take the Trump tax cuts. They fail on so many different levels. (1) They were enacted during a recovery, a time when the US government needed to be building surpluses against the next recession; (2) the economy as a whole did not need them at the time—it was in the midst of one of the longest recoveries on record; (3) they stimulated already frothy markets to greater excesses—the stock market is now posting price-equity ratios (the ratio of the price of a company's stock to its profits or earnings) to unsustainable highs, while the property markets in many urban areas have seen price increases equivalent to those prior to the 2008 crash and a sudden dearth of affordable housing; (4) as a result of all this, they increase the likelihood of a

---

29   United States Treasury, Office of Management and Budget.

forthcoming recession being even worse than it would have been otherwise. Not only this, but the vast majority of taxpayers in this country will see an effect on their pay packets that ranges between nil and minimal—those that benefited most were corporations and the very wealthy.

Why would the Republicans—traditionally the supposed champions of fiscal responsibility—not only endorse but push for such bad policy? Because it was designed to remunerate their winning coalition. Yes, part of Trump's coalition was the disaffected white vote in Middle America, but the overarching Republican coalition was big business. Ever since Citizens United, the Supreme Court ruling that held corporations to be "persons" under the Constitution, the influx of opaque corporate money into the US electoral system has been pervasive—big business and billionaires became the real selectorate, and they needed rewarding.

In short, these tax cuts favoring the wealthy increase the already unsustainable wealth gap in this country. Not since the oil and industrial barons of the early twentieth century has there been such a concentration of wealth in the upper reaches of economic society. This, the increased likelihood of market failure, the lack of government resources to meet the needs of the next recession, and the ballooning of the debt ratio all make overall financial security in America something that is under extreme pressure right now. Woe betide the government that presides over the next collapse.

One way of avoiding—or perhaps mitigating—such blatant use of the tax system to pay off winning coalitions would be to pass legislation (or, even better, a constitutional amendment) that required balancing of the budget over an *aggregate* period. This would state that the federal budget would need to have at least a neutral effect on the national debt (in the absolute) over the specified period. By specifying "in the absolute," such an amendment would guarantee the reduction of the debt over time as a proportion of the economy as a whole. Historically speaking, since the end of World War II, growth periods have averaged around five or six years, while recessions have averaged a year or two. The "aggregate" period in this instance, therefore, could perhaps be ten years or, if you wanted to grant more flexibility to the government, fifteen. Because of the natural perfidy of congressional politicians, I would probably favor the shorter period. To avoid the ability of politicians to move goalposts, I would also suggest that each period be aligned to a specified decade. If we applied this idea to the current decade (starting in 2011), we would have had a couple of years of deficit spending followed by six years (to date) of moderate to strong surpluses. Tax cuts of the Trumpian type would not be allowed until the end of the decade (2020) and/or until aggregate absolute debt had been reduced to what it was in 2011. Exemptions to the rule may be made in the case of war that is declared by Congress, not pursued by the executive branch on its own.

Finally, if government is going to regulate itself financially, then there also need to be clear rules and regulations that govern the financial sector that are designed to maintain financial security. The Dodd-Frank Act was passed in 2010 as a result of the financial meltdown of 2008–9 and was designed to prevent such a meltdown from ever happening again. Among other things, it created the Consumer Financial Protection Bureau as well as what was called the Volcker Rule. This restricted the ability of American banks from making speculative investments on their own behalf that did not benefit their customers. The idea behind the bill was to make banking more transparent and to at least partially restore the divide between speculative banking and consumer banking that had been destroyed in the Clinton era. In early 2018, Congress relaxed some of the key aspects of this act, raising the level of assets needed to comply with its provisions from $50 billion to $250 billion and exempting financial institutions with assets less than $10 billion from the Volcker Rule. Essentially, these provisions gutted the act as it related to smaller and medium-sized institutions, even though, back in the eighties, it was institutions of this size that led to the savings and loan crisis.

There will always be argument over what types and what sizes of financial institutions should be covered by such rules and regulations. The key thing here, however, is that they *are* needed. The banking system has never been able to provide concrete evidence that, in the absence of regulation, it will properly safeguard the interests of the ordinary customer. It did not do so in the Great Depression, during the savings and loan crisis, or during the mortgage meltdown of the last decade. In all cases, the industry looked after its own and in many cases bilked its own depositors. More recently, Wells Fargo has been slammed for creating false accounts in its customers' names and then charging them fees on those accounts.

The ordinary man or woman on the street needs to know their money is safe, their house is safe, and their financial institutions are on their side. In an environment in which plenty of unscrupulous scammers are trying to take people's money from them (from the infamous "grandparent scam" to the likes of Bernie Madoff), and in which recessions happen every ten years or so, people need to be able to trust that they will be OK financially and that, in the event of malfeasance, there is recourse. In other words, they need to be able to live in the absence of fear that their financial security will be ruined.

A Democratic Libertarian government would not necessarily have to be radical in this respect. All it would have to do is put into place the type of robust regulations overseeing the financial industry that were in place before the Clinton era and that served perfectly well for forty years before that. These separated banks' consumer and investment interests, insured customer deposits under the FDIC, and discouraged the creation of "financial instruments" that had the ability to destabilize the entire system. A good example of the latter were the mortgage derivatives by which banks sliced up individual mortgage loans and sold them as securities on the financial markets. When the housing market went sour, nobody could "unslice" the derivatives, creating massive uncertainty in financial circles and eventually bringing down the likes of Lehman and Bear Stearns. All it calls for is a modicum of common sense. Consumer and deposit-based banking should be ring-fenced from all the other types of banking in which financial institutions indulge. The consumer or business that has a checking, savings, or loan account with a financial institution should be confident that the institution in question is not going to gamble with their money and that their money is going to be there for them when they need it.

Finally, let's talk about fraud. Bernie Madoff became the poster boy for Ponzi schemes, but there are numerous other examples of unscrupulous characters who are ready to swindle citizens out of their money. Here in the United States, we are fortunate to have investigative forces and prosecutors who are willing and able to go after these fraudsters and bring them to justice. To a certain extent. A friend of mine was taken for $400,000 and was part of a group of investors that, in total, gave $1 million to someone who turned out to be a con artist. They went to the FBI in Manhattan, who declined to take the case, saying that it was "too small." However, had the jurisdiction been, say, Buffalo, New York, then it would have been large enough to take on and pursue. While it is understandable that Manhattan deals with huge cases of fraud, it is nonetheless not equitable that a group that had been defrauded of so much money would receive attention in one part of the country but not another. The law needs to be applied equally wherever the crime takes place, even if it means adding the necessary resources to juris-dictions where current resources are overwhelmed. No citizen should face a situation in which he or she is in fear of losing their money in one place but not in another. For that is the contract between citizen and state—equal protection under the law.

To this point, we have concentrated on the security of your money—the absence of fear that it will suddenly, and through no fault of your own, disap-pear. But what about the process of making that money? Financial security can only exist in an environment in which there is *economic* security. And, however you cut it, economic security means jobs.

There has been unending argument between economists and other pun-dits about how much a government can either take credit for or be blamed for (un)employment rates and the creation or destruction of jobs in the economy. It is probably true to say that no president can be fully credited for a boom economy, and few can be totally excoriated for a recession. That being said, governments and their policies do affect the overall economy, usually in one of three ways:

1. Through rules and regulations designed to bring about certain results in society or a specific industry

2. Through (often unintended) consequences of economic policy

3. Through government-funded innovation

Republicans and libertarians tend to be united in their hatred of government rules and regulations governing industry. The present administration, combining populism with a very libertarian imagery, has made it a mantra to take down as many regulations as possible. Many of these, despite the imagery, actually serve to pay back the winning coalition. Hence the president nominated as head of the EPA someone who had vowed to destroy the agency and all it stood for. Trump makes no pretense of the fact that this is designed to unleash economic opportunity for oil, coal, and steel. To many in these circles, the idea that government can lay down rules that get in the way of untrammeled commerce is anathema.

While it is true that some regulations can indeed strangle commerce at its roots—the requirement to file many more 1099s as a result of Obamacare, for example—it is also true that governmental regulation can force business to do what it said yesterday was impossible. A great example of this is CAFE (Corporate Average Fuel Economy) standards, which regulate the average fuel consumption of an automotive manufacturer's range of vehicles. The rule is designed to force car and truck manufacturers to increase the fuel efficiency of their products and so reduce pollution and lower our dependence on foreign oil. Despite cries of outrage from the auto industry each time CAFE is made more stringent, the industry always somehow manages to come through. It innovates to get the same power out of its engines while consuming less gas. Similarly, regulations covering flight safety, the manufacture of pharmaceuticals, and safety at work are all there because of a real and present need, and all enrich and protect our lives.

But regulations can have unintended consequences. Take the example of European countries that, wanting to achieve similar reductions in pollution and fuel usage to those proposed by CAFE, started heavily favoring diesel vehicles, most especially at the pump, where diesel attracted less tax per liter than its gasoline equivalent. Within just a few years, diesel-powered new cars overtook their gasoline counterparts to account for over 60 percent of all sales. The premises behind this policy were that new-technology diesels were far cleaner than their predecessors and that they got far better gas mileage. The latter was true but the former not. Thanks to the Volkswagen scandal that started to emerge in 2015, it became clear that not only were modern diesel engines nowhere near as clean as they were purported to be (thanks to huge nitrous oxide emissions in normal driving conditions) but they were also clogging city air with dangerous particulates. This was an unintended and disastrous consequence of European regulations. So now those same regulators are pushing for electric, "zero emission" vehicles as fast as possible, while cities such as London and Paris struggle to clean up their diesel mess. But what if, as an unintended consequence, electric vehicles, packed with lithium ion batteries, spontaneously combust? (This is a hypothetical, by the way. I have no clue if such vehicles will start catching on fire all over the place.)

The point is, government regulations not only need to be very carefully thought through but also need to be used sparingly to achieve real progress in society and the economy. They should also seek to be as neutral as possible in terms of who they favor and those they penalize. And if they do have consequences on a certain portion of the population that turn out to be negative, then carefully thought-out mitigation policies also need to be put into place. As an example, the Obama administration heavily favored the development of alternative energy to mitigate the negative effects of fossil-based fuels on the environment and on general health. From a forward-thinking point of view, this was highly defensible. After all, many

European countries had successfully done the same—France with its reliance on nuclear power and the United Kingdom with its development of wind-powered technologies. But what the Obama administration did *not* do was put into place policies that would ease the transition for those most affected—the coal miners of West Virginia and Kentucky. No wonder they voted for Trump in the next election!

This, however, must fall into the category of "unintended" consequences, even if you could reasonably argue that Obama and his administration were arrogant in not thinking about an entire population and the misery facing them. Yes, this was deplorable, but at least it was not intended. There are other regulations that do intentionally favor certain sections of the population and disadvantage others. Going back to my adopted state of North Carolina, hog farming has become not just big business but huge business. Hog farms either owned by or contractually bound to major companies such as Smithfield (now owned by the Chinese) have become massive enterprises that pollute the environments around them, both in terms of pervasive odor and water quality. Backed by lobbying dollars, the hog-processing combines were able to persuade the Republican legislature to shield them from lawsuits filed by their neighbors that had been increasingly finding against them with significant damages attached. The regulations and protections put in place by the legislature were designed distinctly to favor business over residents, something that government should never do and never could do in a system where the winning coalition is wide. But in North Carolina, the coalition is narrow due to blatant gerrymandering, and so the politicians pay off the members of their coalition (big business) over and above the interests of the nominal selectorate (voters as a whole). So, we have to accept that government regulation of the economy has consequences—sometimes intended for good or ill and sometimes unintended. That is why it should be used sparingly and with the economic well-being of society always front and center.

But it is also true that much of what government does behind the scenes has enormous consequences for the economy, sometimes spanning decades. Take, for example, the development of the ARPANET. Back in the 1930s, a Belgian data expert, Paul Otlet, conceived of the idea of an interconnected library that could be accessed through people's TVs and through which they could send messages to one another. Given that not many people had TVs at the time, the idea remained just that—an idea. It was to remain so for another thirty years until another scientist, J.C.R. Licklider, conceived of similar ideas that he then described as an "Intergalactic Computer Network." In the age of the Cold War, this idea gained momentum within government, particularly at the Advanced Research Projects Agency (ARPA), which promptly recruited Licklider. The result was the ARPANET—networks of computers linked together that could communicate from different locations (in this case, a series of universities). Long story short, with the contribution of a number of highly talented individuals, ARPANET eventually mutated in the late eighties into the Internet that now dominates our lives. In this instance, government instigated innovation that would change lives and boost economic growth, as it has done so many times.

If you think this is an isolated example, then consider this: Government, that institution so reviled by so many on the Libertarian Right (aped by conservatives), has, among other many other breakthroughs, contributed GPS, lactose-free milk, gene therapy, magnetic resonance imaging, LED lighting, and smartphone technology to our modern way of living. Government, pointed in the right direction, can bring resources few others can to bear on problems and issues, and produce amazing innovation. "Government" per se, therefore, should not be a problem for a libertarian. The issue is "pointing it in the right direction." That is what a Democratic Libertarian seeks to do, for the security of all.

If we go back to the premise that it is government's role to ensure financial and economic security for all on an equal playing field, then we come to see that role as being about both providing for security as well as creating the conditions in which the economy—and those within it—can flourish. This does *not* include the government becoming an economic player in and of itself.

When those on the Authoritarian Right hear ideas from the Left about nurturing economic security, the word they usually resort to in order to shoot such ideas down is "socialism." Most who do so have absolutely no idea what this word means, so here, for those who might need a clearer idea of its import, is what "socialism" actually is in a nutshell. Socialism is a system in which the means of production and distribution of goods is collectively owned or owned by the government and, where Marxism is concerned, is a transitional state between capitalism and communism. It has been tried many times and usually been found wanting, whether in the USSR, Venezuela, Zimbabwe, or even the United Kingdom. In the UK, the last manifestation of a quasi-socialist regime was in the 1960s and 1970s. Entire industries were government-owned, including coal and steel, as well as individual companies deemed "too important to fail." These last included most of the motorcycle industry as well as the British Motor Holding Company, later to become British Leyland. At one point, this was the second largest automotive firm in the world, second only to General Motors. It included such famous brands as Austin, Morris, Wolseley, Riley, Triumph, MG, Rover, Land Rover, Jaguar, and Austin-Healey. State ownership of such a major organization proved to be a complete disaster, culminating in the firm's collapse and its eventual sale back into the private sector as a shadow of its former self. Today, just two brands still exist, both in foreign ownership—Mini (the spiritual successor of Austin and Morris) and Jaguar–Land Rover. The steel and coal industries did not fare that well either.

In every economy where a socialist government has taken control of the means of production and/or distribution, the result has been catastrophic. Why? Because governments and politicians are not business people. They do and decide things for different reasons and by different standards than those used by business. They don't know how to run industries and companies in a world in which their competitors are professional capitalists. It's as simple as that. Ask President Maduro how the Venezuelan oil monopoly is faring against the likes of Exxon or Shell.

This is why the Right loves to throw the word "socialism" around whenever describing anything vaguely "left." It is a word that spells failure, even if the Right actually doesn't know what it means. But that is not what Democratic Libertarianism means. This is not a socialist dogma. Indeed, it is not a dogma or an ideology at all. It is a framework in which people and government can work together, with security being the primary basis of all that governs society and rule making. As such, a Democratic Libertarian economic framework is one in which businesses can invest for healthy returns on both capital and labor and in which both shareholders and labor can share equitably in these returns. It is a framework in which simplicity in rule making and in tax laws allows for transparency in investment while ensuring that the economy as a whole does not tilt toward an imbalance that endangers the security of society as a whole. Indeed, it is designed to enhance that security while still allowing for the innovation and risk-taking that has made the American economy unique for all these years.

To be in business today is not an undertaking for the faint of heart. Market conditions and technology change so fast that companies must have the maximum flexibility to respond, whether that response is to invest in more technology, change their entire business model, or outsource some operations to places other than the United States.

Government interference in the workings of the economy often has unintended consequences, which is why government should restrict its role in the economy to ensuring that it is balanced (assuring long-term stability for all), is used sparingly when needed to correct imbalances, and promotes innovation. Beyond this, however, government can also lay down conditions in the background that *enable* economic growth and individual financial security. It can do this through the provision of critically needed training, incentive schemes to invest in certain activities or locations, the building and maintenance of infrastructure (something that is woefully lacking at present), and incubating innovation. Even more fundamentally, it can lay down the conditions for an educated and healthy workforce—two things that are vital to a high-performance economy in the twenty-first century.

Financial security is a basic Maslovian need

Capitalism has been proven to be the only modern-day system that can provide financial security, but capitalism needs governmental oversight to prevent it from going off the rails and damaging financial security.

Basic reforms are needed

Rebalance the system to give capital and labor an equal say

Revert to real Keynsianism and save for rainy days

Simplify the tax system—three bands, no deductions

Balance aggregate budgets over specified period of time

Reduce and eventually eliminate sales tax

Prosecute financial corruption to the fullest extent

Simplify and segregate the banking system

Use regulation to ensure security, not favor special interests

12

An Educated Society Is a Secure Society

No society can provide economic or financial security without educational security. Simply put, if you are not educated for the jobs that are out there, you will not get a job that will afford you financial security for the rest of your life. For the educational system, this is a huge challenge, given the very rapid changes in the economy that are happening all around us. In the last forty years, the United States has moved from being a manufacturing economy to a service-based one to one that is based on data and analytics. In a 2016 study by the McKinsey Global Institute, it was estimated that the US would be short of 250,000 data scientists by 2024. Education is critical in closing that gap. As Michael Chui, a partner at McKinsey Global Institute, put it, "The ability to understand what probability means is now a basic fact of life. It has tremendous implications for us as workers and citizens." But if you are an educational establishment, this means you have to be able to turn on a dime, retool your curriculum, and rethink the structure of your teaching staff. For this, you need budget funds, which are often severely lacking in many school districts around this country.

For a country as rich as the United States is, our record in education is appalling. Every three years, the Organisation for Economic Co-operation and Development (OECD) sponsors a cross-national test called PISA (Programme for International Student Assessment). In 2015, the latest year for which data are available, the United States scored thirty-eighth out of seventy-one countries participating in math and twenty-fourth in science.[30] We were also twenty-fourth in reading. This in a world where educational achievement in math and science especially is critical to national and individual success. (By the way, many of those Left Libertarian societies that we found were richer and happier than we are also happened to score much better on education as well—including Canada, New Zealand, Australia, the Netherlands, Denmark, Norway, and Sweden.)

How on earth does the world's richest nation fail so dismally in educating its future generations? It's not that we fail universally—our elementary students fare much better, and sixteen out of the top twenty-five universities in the world are American.[31] Out of these, ten are private and six public. It seems that where we fail our students the most is in their secondary education. Why should this be? There are a few reasons that fall into three categories: financial, structural, and ideological.

The first of these is perhaps the most cynical. Education *financing* can be squeezed because teachers and children are easy targets. In times of financial difficulty, it is easy for states to put a freeze on teacher salaries, school budgets, and educational investment. In times of plenty, it is more politically expedient to give tax cuts than to restore salaries, budget, and investment. Time was, the local teacher was held in the highest esteem in any local community. Today, she earns a salary that, even if she has a master's degree and has been teaching for thirty years, still lags significantly behind that of a first-year data scientist. The average teacher in 2017 earned a salary of $58,950, which was nearly 2 percent *lower* than in 1999. In Arizona, Colorado, Indiana, Michigan,

---

30 Pew Research Center, February 2017.
31 Times Higher Education, World University Rankings 2020.

and North Carolina, the drop in average salary over that period of time was in double digits (above 10 percent).[32] Why? Simply because they could. Not only were salaries cut but so were school and district budgets as a whole, eliminating scores of programs such as sports, art, drama, and after-school events. Additionally, most teachers dig into their own pockets to an average tune of $500 a year to pay for supplies for their classrooms where budgets have been cut. All this while working two jobs where many are concerned, just to make ends meet. How did we get from teacher as revered member of the community to teacher as piggy bank? Through sheer fiscal cynicism— legislators spotted a soft target for saving money (often to give away to the wealthier through tax cuts), and they went with it. Thankfully, teachers across the country seem to be saying "we've had enough" and are striking and rallying to force their state legislators into at least partially remedying the situation. But the ugly truth is, if you downgrade education as a fiscal priority, outcomes will suffer, no matter how many tests you mandate in the place of funding.

Perhaps an even bigger issue, however, is the structural one of educational funding. More than half of the funds that go toward education in this country are sourced from property taxes. There is sound historical reasoning for this. In the pioneering and colonial days, education was very much a local concern. Your township or village had its schoolhouse and teacher, paid for by local funding—mainly property tax. As America has mutated from rural to urban to suburban to exurban, this system of funding education has survived, leading to extraordinary imbalances in the funding of schooling between richer and poorer neighborhoods. If you live in Bloomfield Hills, a suburb of Detroit, you are likely to have much more funding for your schools and much better schools as a result than if you live in central Detroit, where the reverse is going to be true. Since much of the difference

32   Kudos, though, to California, DC, Massachusetts, Montana, North Dakota, Vermont, and Wyoming, where the opposite was true. Average salaries increased by double digits.

between such neighborhoods can also be traced to race, it is also true that the education between whites and blacks is hugely different. It was thought that the landmark Supreme Court case *Brown v. Board of Education* would deal with this once and for all, but the truth in modern-day America is that schools are once again as segregated as before. Which means that the method of funding those schools still is supremely important.

America likes to think of itself as an "exceptional" nation, and in this it is. It is the only developed Western nation in which education funding is still locally, not nationally, determined. And it is the only one in which the effect of being a minority student does not affect the funding accorded to a school. As an example, in the Netherlands, school funding is a function of central government and is based on numbers of students enrolled.[33] This is then adjusted by the economic class of the children concerned and their race—a policy designed to lift those children out of poverty. Similar policies exist throughout the Western developed world.

So, American education faces a double whammy: States have used it as a piggy bank during bad times and good while the core structure of its funding is based in a system of two hundred years ago that just happens to keep the poor and minorities "in their place."

A third issue contributes to American education's poor performance on the international stage: ideology. For some unfathomable reason, education has been equated by those on the Right with elitism. To be called "elite" today is one of the worst insults the Right can throw at you. Universities are seen as being "elite" or, even worse, "elitist." Educators—especially in higher learning—are seen as being "elite," left wing, and untrustworthy. Even Republican columnists such as David Brooks of the *New York Times* or George Will are being labeled "elitist" for speaking out against the Trump administration. What does this new smear actually mean? At its base, it means that these are people who are antipopulist, people who think things through

---

33   ASCD, *Educational Leadership*, January 2012.

rather than rely on gut instinct to make their political decisions. But it goes deeper than this. There is a distrust of educated people because those people lacked empathy for and with the very visceral woes of the same people with whom Trump connected. They talked up and invested in alternative energy while ignoring the plight of those in the coal industry who saw their liveli- hoods evaporate before their very eyes. They entered into trade agreements that disadvantaged many industries (even if they were on balance good for the economy as a whole) while ignoring the consequences of what they had put into place. The people who did all of this were all educated at Harvard, Princeton, Yale, or similar institutions. They were the educated; they were the "elite." How easy is it then to carry that contempt for education into the mainstream? Why bother to dedicate resources to education if all that does is produce people who ultimately will screw you? In a state like North Carolina, where the majority of the legislature hails from rural areas, such arguments carry a lot of weight.

Yet, all logic points to education being one of the most important invest- ments a modern society can make. How can we move from a society in which it is devalued to one where it is at the center of future success? The current administration's solution is to lump the Education and Labor Departments together, treating education as an adjunct of producing a pop- ulation fit for the workforce.

I would argue that a more radical solution is necessary—one that rec- ognizes that both education and health care are two of the most important investments a country makes if it wishes to guarantee future success. First of all, the funding of education would need to change radically. In other, less federal, Western systems, education funding is a function of central govern- ment, paid for out of income taxes. We have to recognize that in the federal system of the United States, this would not be possible—at least not beyond the boundaries that currently exist between federal and state governments. But, at the state level, it is already partially a central responsibility. On a state-by-state basis, the *mechanism* of funding needs to change, moving away from localized property taxes toward a dependence on statewide income taxes. After that, the *distribution* of funding also has to change to one that is not only dependent on student numbers but also weighted toward poorer neighborhoods (regardless of race). The Dutch system, which has produced one of the most educated populations in the world, would not be a bad starting place.

Another great source of contention in the American system is what is referred to as the "voucher" system. Proposed primarily by Republican administrations, this allows families to take the money that would be spent on their child in the public education system and apply it to an education in the private system. Proponents claim that this provides freedom of choice in educational alternatives to parents while ensuring that they and their children can escape underperforming schools and school districts. Opponents claim that such a system drains money from the public system and ensures that underperforming schools will, in fact, fail. Federally, there is no right established to the receipt of an education, a fact that was upheld in a 1973 Supreme Court ruling that firmly placed the responsibility of educational policy with the individual states.[34]

Education is indeed addressed in each of the fifty states' constitutions, but in ways that vary considerably. However, what *all* of them do is guarantee the provision of free public education—this is the common building block. Most do not address the existence of a parallel system of private tuition, nor do they consider the interaction between the two systems or any interweaving of their funding. This is left in most cases to the legislatures to work out.

From a purely constitutional point of view, proponents of vouchers are probably strictly within the bounds of the law—they are providing and funding education for the public while at the same time still maintaining a public school system. But if that system were to collapse as a result of the diversion of funds to private schools, then they would be in contravention

---

34   *San Antonio Independent School District v. Rodriguez*, 1973.

of their constitutional mandates. This, then, becomes a gray area—to what extent can public money be used to provide private education before doing so violates the constitutional requirement to provide "effective" (a word used in many of the states) public schools? Again, I would argue that this comes back to the system of funding. A system based on property taxes is bound to produce schools and, indeed, entire school districts that fail. Whereas one that is based on income tax proceeds and that actively directs funding to the less fortunate among us would negate the need for vouchers. That need only exists to allow parents of children in underperforming and underresourced areas to escape the system as it is now. It preserves that system (while destroying those same underresourced areas) by relying on the libertarian veneer of "choice." But a choice that is made necessary by a political system intent on destruction of public education is a false choice. Better by far to alter radically the system of education funding to ensure that success is available to all.

This is not to say that choice should be taken away from parents entirely. The present system in many states (and countries) whereby your children go to schools designated by where you live is autocratic in the extreme. Why should politicians or bureaucrats tell you where you can and cannot send your children to school? This is the authoritarian version of local government, where you as the citizen have limited, if any, choice. Worse than this, it leads to gaming of the system. Some parents, whose income allows them to do so, choose a particular district in which to live while their children are in elementary or middle school and then move so as to be able to get their kids into high schools with a better reputation. As a result, the housing market is distorted by educational needs, forcing house prices up in areas with "good" schools and depressing those in other areas. The more this happens, the more only those that can afford these elevated prices can get their offspring into the schools of their choice. The ultimate result: a boost to the widening of the wealth gap and a worsening of the ability of the poor to escape from poverty. And, even worse, a hardening of the sclerotic arteries of economic mobility.

It used to be said that, in America, you could achieve anything with hard work. Not any longer. Today, America ranks among the lowest of Western developed nations in terms of economic and social mobility.[35] If you are born in the bottom quintile of economic households, you are likely to stay there. If you are born in the top quintile, you are likely to stay there as well. Which countries rank top in the economic mobility rankings? Denmark, Norway, Finland, and Canada—those Democratic Libertarian nations that are not only among the richest in the world but the happiest. How strange.

With a funding system in place, based on income tax and not property tax, it is not impossible to imagine an education system in which teachers regain their status in society (with pay that reflects this). Indeed, we can now imagine a form of education that moves away from standardized testing and multiple choice to real, child-centered learning, emphasizing equally the careers for which we are preparing children and the training of their minds to be able to think, create, and manage for themselves.

It is interesting to me that in preschool and kindergarten, we encourage child creativity. But once we get them into the education system proper, the emphasis quickly changes to conformity—you behave in a certain way, learn in a certain way, and strive to perform well on your tests. The whole person—the person whose development is enriched by art, drama, debate, and philosophy—is squeezed like a round peg into a square hole of conformity. Today, only where funding is privately sourced (fees and endowments in the private sector) does this type of education survive. We measure children and schools alike on their test scores and not on the person they have become. And when universities choose students on the latter rather than the former, all hell breaks loose from those with 1600 SAT scores who did not get in to the school of their choice while a more rounded kid from the projects did. (Unless they are sports athletes. That's OK, because that means millions of dollars to the college's bottom line.)

---

35   Pew Charitable Trusts Economic Mobility Project, July 2015.

So let's imagine a different education manifesto, all the while remembering that this is one of the most important *investments* that a country can make:

· Education funding becomes a responsibility solely for the states but comes out of income, not property, taxes. A statutory minimum of a state's budget would be devoted to education—a minimum that could not be altered even in bad times.

· District and school funding is allocated on headcount and then *upweighted* based on parental income.

· Operating costs are treated differently from investment spending—just as is the case in business.

· Private education continues to coexist with public but is not funded by it.

· Teachers are paid salaries that reflect their importance to society.

· Curricula reflect the need to teach the whole child, not to prep the poor kid to be an automaton test-taker.

· Schools and districts are judged not by the test scores of their pupils. Instead, they are judged by their *output* in terms of the success of their students—how many graduated, how many went on to university, how many are in jobs, what are those jobs, what were their starting salaries, and what have their alumni achieved for society?

This last point may seem a little strange, but it is how the best schools around the world judge themselves. Until recently, I chaired the alumni association of my old high school, a place of learning that educates the whole child and gives every single one of its nine hundred students the chance to discover who they really are. What they want to know above all is, did we give this child the best possible start in life? Did we set them up for success? Did they achieve that success? And what have they done to give back to society? Oh, and by the way, this school deliberately serves the most disadvantaged children in society—those from poor neighborhoods, broken homes, and dysfunctional families.

Only when we think like this will we place education where it should be: right at the center of society. There is only one other aspect of societal security that should occupy that space alongside education—and that is health.

Education is an investment, not a cost. A fundamental right, not a privilege.

Fund education appropriately and make it a fiscal priority

Move funding from property taxes to state income taxes

Distribute the funding on the basis of need, not wealth

Simplify the tax system—three bands, no deductions

Set a statutory minimum of state budgets that go toward education

Allow private and public systems to co-exist, but only public schools to be funded by the state

Raise teacher salaries to reflect their importance and expertise

13

The Health and Wellness Investment

Our borders are secure, and we are safe as a nation. We are individually secure and need not fear crime or personal aggression. We are well educated. We have good jobs and are financially secure. But none of this counts for much if we don't have health security.

In Russia, for example, where national defense is a priority, crime is relatively contained, and the economy is sustained by oil and gas, the average life expectancy of a man is just 66 years.[36] Most of this is due to alcoholism, which the Russian government is trying to combat with some success. By contrast, the top five nations in terms of male life expectancy are Switzerland, Iceland, Australia, Sweden, and Israel, all topping 80 years or more.[37] The United States ranks thirty-second at 76.9 years. What's worrisome is that after years of steady increases in life expectancy in the US, the last three years for which we have data (2013–2016) have shown a decline,[38] with

---

36   Russian Federal Statistics Service, 2015.

37   World Health Organization, 2015.

38   CNN, 2017.

increases in deaths due to opioid overdose, Alzheimer's disease, and suicide being cited as the primary causes.

The United States spent $3.3 trillion on health care in 2016.[39] This equates to $10,348 per person and accounts for 17.9 percent of gross domestic product. By contrast, comparable countries spent half this amount—and the gap in spending has been widening almost constantly for the last fifty years.

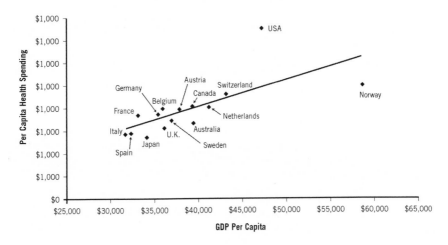

Per Capita Health Spending in Major Economies

Source: Kaiser Family Foundation

Of this, 32 percent was spent on hospital stays, 20 percent on physicians and clinics, and 10 percent on prescription drugs. Just over a third was spent by the government (Medicare, Medicaid, and the VA) and a third through private insurance. Overall, 91.2 percent of the population was insured one way or another, while in comparable countries,[40] all of which offer "socialized" or single-payer medical systems, that figure was 99.9 percent.[41]

---

39   Center for Medicare and Medicare Services, 2018.

40   France, Australia, Japan, Sweden, the Netherlands, Austria, Germany, and the United Kingdom.

41   Kaiser Family Foundation, OECD, 2015.

So, we spend double the amount per capita on health care compared to our peer countries. What do we get for our money? According to the Kaiser Family Foundation, the OECD, and the London School of Economics (from whom all these statistics were gathered), the answer is "not nearly enough." Mortality rates in the United States are higher than in other comparable countries, especially where diseases of the circulatory, respiratory, and nervous systems are concerned. Deaths from mental and behavioral disorders are also increasing more than in other nations, especially dementia. But perhaps most worrying of all is the fact that the US ranks highest among all comparable countries for "deaths amenable to health care"—that is, deaths due to diseases that are controllable in a prevention-oriented system. These include congestive heart failure, asthma, and diabetes. But it's not all doom and gloom. The American health system fares better on mortality rates for breast and colorectal cancer, and you are much less likely in the US to suffer from postoperative clots (pulmonary embolism or deep vein thrombosis) than you are in other countries.

Many would argue that the raw statistics paint an unfair picture of the United States when it comes to health care. Indeed, Tim Norbeck, CEO of the Physicians Foundation, writing in *Forbes*, argued forcibly that the stats were not comparing apples to apples.[42] He made a number of arguments, all of which have some validity:

- The rate of poverty in the United States (at 12.7 percent of the population when Norbeck was writing) is much higher than in the comparable countries. So, of course, there will be higher incidence of diseases such as congestive heart failure and diabetes, as these people cannot afford a healthy lifestyle. Unsaid in his argument: and they can't afford health insurance.

---

42   Gary Price and Tim Norbeck. "US Health Outcomes Compared to Other Countries Are Misleading." *Forbes*, April 9, 2018.

- The US is a much bigger country than the others, so the administrative costs of health care are that much higher. On a per capita basis, I am not sure that argument really holds water. But if he had said that dealing with an entire other layer—the insurance industry—that does not exist in these other nations adds administrative complexity, I could buy that.

- The medical liability environment in the US is much more hostile than elsewhere, so doctors prescribe tests and procedures that are generally unnecessary in order to protect themselves from lawsuits should anything go wrong. Definitely true.

- The cost of pharmaceuticals in America is among the highest in the world, leading to spending on drugs that is twice as high as in all of the eleven comparable countries. The pharma industry says this is due to artificial caps on pricing in other countries, leaving the US to bear the burden of developing very costly drugs. This may or may not be true.

- "High-margin, high-volume" procedures such as knee replacements are far less frequent in single-payer economies than in the US. He takes pride in this, pointing to ninety-year-olds playing tennis again, which is great but seems to be at the cost of basic health care elsewhere in the system (e.g., the poor).

- Norbeck also points out that America's less-than-stellar performance in terms of life expectancy is due to the higher incidence in this country of suicides, fatal car wrecks, gun homicides, and obesity leading to diabetes, which (to a certain extent) is true.

Norbeck is writing from the point of view of protecting American physicians, whose overall reputation he fears will be tarnished by an uninformed reading of the statistics. This is an absolutely understandable position to take and is not lacking validity, at least to some degree. But what he appears to do at the same time is to skate over *why* some of these mitigating circumstances exist. *Why* is our poverty rate so high? *Why* do we have such a complicated health care and payment system that adds to administrative cost? *Why* are there so many uninsured? *Why* is medical liability so out of control? *Why* does big pharma accept price caps elsewhere and expect the American consumer to foot the bill? To me, all of these questions point the finger at a broken system of authoritarian government that is content to pay off its small real selectorate by ignoring these very real symptoms of malaise in one of the two most important investment areas for a successful society—health.

Even if we accept Norbeck's arguments, there are some statistics provided by Kaiser and the OECD that cannot be explained away so easily. Why does the US, for example, have fewer doctors than comparable countries (2.6 per head of population as compared to 3.4 in the other nations)? Why does it take longer in America to get to see a doctor? Why are there more errors in surgery, medication, and lab tests here than elsewhere?[43] And why do we have the highest rate of deaths from diseases that were amenable to preventive health care?

As persuasive as Norbeck's arguments are, the bottom line still remains that we spend twice as much on health care as any other Western nation and that the outcomes are mediocre at best. From an economic perspective, this is not all bad. After all, pharmaceuticals and health care in general form a booming sector of the economy, employing millions and adding to its payrolls all the time. Alongside the Swiss, British, Germans, and French, the US dominates the pharmacological and biogen industries of the world. They are highly innovative, provide high-paying jobs, and contribute massively to GDP and the balance of trade. Add to this the insurance industry, and we now have a sector that is the largest employer in the United States.[44] What's more, health care jobs are projected to account for one-third of all new jobs created in the next decade.

---

43   Kaiser Family Foundation, 2018.
44   Bureau of Labor Statistics, 2019.

So we can rightfully say that this is an incredibly important sector for the future of the American economy.

And yet, ironically, part of the reason for the health care and insurance industries being so important to the economy is that the current system is, if not broken, severely damaged. If we are spending twice what other countries do on health care and yet are not getting the outcomes that they do, then we can only surmise that our overall return on investment of this part of our economy is not that great. Which begs the question—if we were able to divert at least some of these resources to other sectors while improving outcomes at the same time, would that not be a better allocation of our national resources?

In addition to this question, we also need to look more closely at the dark side of the equation. Despite all this spending, the system as currently constructed does not contribute to either individual or societal security. Indeed, numerous aspects of it lead us to feel *insecure*, inducing fear and uncertainty. In our Democratic Libertarian world, that is a complete betrayal of government's contract with its citizens to provide the second Maslovian level of personal security. Consider the following:

1. *Insurance premiums.* In a society that spends so much on health care, there has to be a way to pay for it. In the United States, this happens by way of health insurance providers. Not only does this insert a level of complexity into the health care ecosystem not present elsewhere in the Western world, it is expensive. While Obamacare attempted to mitigate this inconvenient truth, it still perpetuated the insurance system and indeed, arguably, worsened it. There are three reasons why private health insurance contributes to a decline in personal and societal security:

   ◦ As health care costs rise (due to all the factors we have outlined so far in this chapter), so do the liabilities of insurance companies who have to cover them. The natural human and corporate response to this is to mitigate exposure to these costs, leading to insurance companies increasing deductibles while reducing the conditions that they will actually cover. In many cases, this means that people who think they are insured lose most of their net wealth before insurance actually kicks in (if it does at all).

∘ The main channel for the sale of health insurance is employers. Most companies above a certain size offer health benefits that are bought from a health insurer. But, as costs rise, employers become less and less willing or able to foot the entire bill and so push more of the costs on to the employees while offering less in the way of coverage and benefits. The employee is now held hostage to not one but two for-profit entities for whom their health insurance costs are a major element determining corporate profitability. The actual access of the employee to affordable health care now becomes something that is secondary to the profits of both employer and insurance company.

∘ If you are not lucky enough to be an employee of a company offering health benefits, you have to buy your health insurance on the open market. Here, premiums can take up a very sizable proportion of take-home income—and even then, with high deductibles, not cover the basics of health care. No wonder many of the self-employed opt not to buy health coverage.

Obamacare tried to mitigate many of these issues, especially some of the most egregious, such as noncoverage of preexisting conditions. It also was an unqualified success in reducing the number of uninsured through providing premium subsidies and extending Medicare in those states willing to do so. However, the law of unintended consequences also came into play and, in many states, trumped the good intentions of the Affordable Care Act. By opening up the market to previously uninsured people with preexisting conditions that had hitherto gone untreated, Obamacare increased the cost burden on the system. The idea that the addition of previously uninsured healthy young people into the system would counterbalance this did not work out as planned. Premiums rose, plans became scarcer as insurers left markets, and the system became unwieldy.

The basic problem here is that Obamacare tried to put lipstick on the American health care pig. A system that relies on a chain of for-profit organizations to underscore the health of a nation is just not going to work. Profit and return to shareholders will always come before equitable health outcomes, no matter how much the players protest otherwise.

2. *Where serious becomes catastrophic.* It's pretty serious when your doctor says to you, "I'm afraid it's cancer." Your life gets turned upside down, your life expectancy comes into question, and you face horrifically difficult questions around what routes your treatment and care should take. If you opt for aggressive treatment, such as chemo or radiation, not only do you become incapacitated for months on end, rendering you incapable of working or earning an income, but you commit yourself to hugely expensive therapies that may or may not work. While in many cases you may be covered by insurance, there may also be large deductibles as well as payout caps that, in the end, leave you with huge bills for your care at the exact moment when your income dries up. For far too many people who are lucky enough to survive such treatment, the end result is bankruptcy, the loss of their home, the loss of their job, and, potentially, life on the street. In any modern Western democracy, this is just unacceptable.

3. *The uninsured burden on your back.* Depending on when you measure it, some thirty million people remain uninsured in this country. Obamacare tried—and succeeded—in bringing this number down, but it seems the current administration is content to see it rise again. Whatever the number, the truth is that the uninsured are not a superhealthy segment of the population because they never get sick. On the

contrary, the majority of them are people so poor that they cannot afford health insurance (with a few right-wing libertarians who say "just leave me to die"). When serious illness hits these people, they go to the emergency room of their nearest hospital, where they have the right to be treated whether or not they have insurance. Even if they are billed for their treatment, very few will have the resources to pay, which means the hospital itself picks up the tab. This gets factored into the normal running costs of a hospital, which translates into the costs that the hospital charges to the insurance company, which increases the premiums you and I pay for our policies. While some on the Left may see this as a worthy transfer of resources from rich to poor, I would suggest that it is a very clumsy and inefficient way to ensure equity in both access to and financing of a health system.

Here is the final kicker in this sorry tale—one that will probably turn any feelings of incredulity you might have right now into ones of outright outrage: You, the American taxpayer, pay more for government spending on health care than any other comparable country in the OECD study. Indeed, in many instances, you pay more for government spending on health care than many other developed Western nations spend on health care in its entirety, both public and private! Tax-funded expenditure on health care in America amounted in 2013 to 64.3 percent of all spending on health (private and public)—the equivalent of $5,960 per year on every single man, woman, and child in this country.[45] Where does that money come from? From every single taxpayer in the nation. And where does it go to? To the elderly, the poor, and veterans. In this antisocialist country, if you as a politician try to mess with any of Medicare, Medicaid, or the VA, you are touching a third rail. The same goes for Social Security. The Right call these

---

45 David Himmelstein and Steffie Woolhandler. "The Current and Projected Taxpayer Shares of US Health Costs." *American Journal of Public Health,* March 2016.

"entitlements" in a sneering sort of way and would love to see them pared back. The electorate, which would rather die than be called "socialist," would rather die than see this happen.

So, let's get this straight. As a nation we spend more of our wealth on health care than does any other country—twice as much, in fact. As taxpayers, we pay more than others and then are expected to lay out even more through private insurance policies. Health care costs more here than anywhere else, and yet outcomes for patients lag behind the rest of the world in key and important areas. What's more, some twenty million to thirty million (depending on who you believe) remain uninsured, while those that are insured often find their policies are close to worthless in covering all but the most catastrophic circumstances—and sometimes not even those. People who fall through that particular trapdoor can lose everything, finding themselves homeless and bankrupt. This is the richest nation on the planet, and yet the one bedrock security that a healthy society needs—absence of fear of the consequences of ill health—is denied us. It is not just shocking; it is a dereliction of duty on the part of elected politicians in the world's biggest democracy. The average German, Brit, or Scandinavian looks at America and scratches their head in wonder. President Trump is fond of saying America is the laughingstock of the world— this is one area in which that would indeed be true, and yet he and his cohorts in Washington have failed dismally to do anything about it.

But, in truth, this is no laughing matter. One of the most scandalous and yet under-reported aspects of our health system is the almost total lack of access to health care in many rural areas. The federal government itself admits that fifty million rural Americans live in "healthcare shortage areas."[46] Much of this lack is found on Native American reservations, but it is also prevalent in white rural communities. For example, Tennessee has lost 14 percent of its rural physicians and 18 percent of its rural hospitals in the last

---

46   Health Resources and Services Administration, October 2019.

ten years, and two and a half million Tennessee residents are now left with insufficient access to health care.[47] The only form of health care access that many people get in such areas is pop-up volunteer traveling clinics that operate out of schools and other public facilities on an infrequent basis.

What can be done about it? In the type of world I am describing in this book—a Democratic Libertarian world—the responsibility of government is to set the framework by which society is secure and individuals live in the absence of fear. From there on in, government moves out of the way to allow citizens to live freely and to reach their own levels of self-esteem and self-actualization. Health forms one of the bedrocks of a secure framework and is vital for people to flourish economically and socially. As oxymoronic as it may seem, therefore, in this type of libertarian society it is indeed government's responsibility to ensure a system of health care that is affordable, accessible, efficient, and effective. In all the other countries we have studied so far in this book, that system is encapsulated in two short words: *single payer.*

Cue apoplexy and aneurisms from the Authoritarian Right. Cue their alternative names for such a system—"socialist" and "socialized." Cue frenzied discussions of "death panels," Big Government making decisions on your treatment, and hospitals with pigs running amok in the corridors. None of that is true, of course, but it makes a wonderful narrative with which to scare the bejesus out of Joe Voter.

The United Kingdom has had a single-payer system since just after the Second World War. Funded by taxes, it offers free health care to every citizen in the country, from doctor visits to vaccinations to home care for the chronically ill to hospitalization. It has had its ups and downs and is today, under a right-wing government, underfunded, but it performs. Health outcomes in the UK of the types we were discussing earlier are routinely superior to those in the US. Hospitals are modern, and the country has

---

47   *Washington Post,* June 24, 2019.

a flourishing pharmaceutical sector and is at the leading edge of medical science.

Let's visit one local hospital in particular—Salisbury District Hospital in the sleepy medieval city of Salisbury in southern England. There is nothing particularly special about this hospital—it was built about fifteen years ago, has a modern, cheerful feel about it, is spotlessly clean, and has an excellent medical and nursing staff. It's not a renowned teaching hospital like Johns Hopkins in Baltimore or St. Thomas' in London. It's just a local hospital. On March 4, 2018, two new patients were admitted—Sergei Skripal, a former KGB officer who was a double agent for the British, and his daughter (visiting from Russia), Yulia. They had been discovered semiconscious on a public bench in a popular shopping district in the city and were unresponsive. What nobody knew at the time was they had been poisoned by a virulent nerve agent developed by the Russians in the Cold War called Novichok. How many hospitals in the world do you think could have worked that out as fast as Salisbury District Hospital did? Or could actually save both the lives of two people from something that was designed to be 100 percent deadly? I am not saying that every hospital in Britain could have performed as this one did—and I do admit they got a lot of help from a government chemical weapons laboratory nearby. All I am saying is that this is a long way from the "fake news" stories dredged up by the Authoritarian Right when the issue of single-payer systems comes up for discussion. Talk to a German, a French person, a Dane, or a New Zealander and you will hear similar stories about their systems too. And here's one final interesting thought: The British love to moan about the National Health Service (NHS), but they are at one and the same time intensely proud of it. For any politician, right or left, to tinker with or suggest replacing this system is to touch the third rail of British politics. It is fatal.

How does a single-payer system work? First, the source of funding is uniform. Generally speaking, it comes from general taxation as well as a specific tax designed to fund the overall health system. This means taxpayers are by far the primary source of money. In some systems there are discrete charges for certain services (for example, dentistry or eye care), but these usually amount to a tiny proportion of the overall budget. That money is then disbursed to local health authorities who decide the priorities in funding, dependent on their own demographics and circumstances. Local authorities receive money based both on headcount and on demographic adjustments—for example, an area with an overweighting of the elderly might receive more, as may a poorer area where maintenance of good health in a difficult economic environment becomes a priority. One major misconception is that central government gets to decide how the money is spent. In most systems, this is a local decision using local knowledge.

The second key feature of a single-payer system is that the central government gets to negotiate with pharmaceutical companies on the price of drugs. The sheer buying power of the government means that drug prices are generally kept at a lower level than when a system of private insurers is involved. One of the weirder aspects of the American system is that Medicare cannot carry out such negotiations and so reduce the cost of drugs to its recipients. Indeed, the secretary of health and human services is *explicitly* barred by law from doing so! In a single-payer system, this is one of *the* primary advantages that the government holds.

From a citizen's point of view, the advantages are many. All health care is free at point of service, so you are not going to lose your home or go bankrupt as a result of the costs of your treatment. Neither will you be denied coverage or treatment if you have a preexisting condition. Indeed, since the condition would have been preexisting within the same system, it becomes a moot point. You have the condition; it will be treated. What's more, in many countries your treatment will be seamlessly connected to social services aimed at making your life as livable as possible while you battle or recuperate from your illness. As an example, my own father, diagnosed at eighty-two with fibrosis of the lung, discovered on his discharge from the hospital that his bathroom had been remodeled to make it easier for him to bathe and that a care worker would visit him each morning and evening to help him with dressing and undressing. All this was free of charge at the point of service.

This is not to say there are not drawbacks in a single-payer system. Indeed, in any system, public or private, access to health care has to be limited in some fashion or another. Most countries cannot afford to provide unlimited access for every single kind of procedure—there would not be enough money to go around. Such differences that exist are in *how* access is limited. In the United States, it is through money—you can or cannot afford health insurance, or the insurance you have will impose things such as deductibles and procedures that are not covered. In a single-payer system, there are two levers usually used: time and availability. Most such systems will not offer elective cosmetic surgery, for example. If you want that facelift, you would need to go to the private sector. In other areas—for example, hip or knee replacements—you may need to wait a few months before being scheduled for surgery. In all cases, the urgent will take precedence over all other needs for intervention. For insured Americans who are used to getting what they want medically quickly, this would probably be an irritant, but maybe their irritation would be assuaged by the fact that there would be no huge hospital bills to look forward to post-surgery!

Why would a single-payer health system be preferable to what we have now?

- Everyone would be covered, regardless of wealth or income.

- Everyone would be covered for the same things—no more differential insurance policies based on cost, deductible, and coverage exceptions.

- This would eliminate the need for thousands of nonmedical people (insurers) making health decisions on your behalf.

- The elimination of private insurance companies in the mix would take the "for-profit" element out of the equation, thereby reducing costs. An entire bureaucratic layer would be removed from the system; workers in these companies would receive government assistance in finding new careers and opportunities, some of them within the single-payer system.

· The anxiety felt by millions of Americans about health and its linkage to financial well-being or ruin would be removed. A level of essential security would be restored to the national framework.

Understand that establishing a single-payer public system of health provision would not automatically eliminate a private health sector for those who prefer to pay directly for their treatment and care. In all of the comparable countries in the OECD study, there exists a parallel system run on private insurance lines. People can opt out of the public system and pay reduced taxes (they still pay *some* tax, however, on the principle that health is a public as well as a private good). In most cases, the two systems thrive alongside each other.

There is one final aspect of health care that needs to be examined before turning to other elements of security in our society, and that is care for the elderly. The demographics of the developed world are changing dramatically. As medicine and clean(er) environments have extended life spans significantly over the last hundred years, our populations have been growing older. The current late baby boomers, together with generations in their forties and fifties, are the first in the modern world to combine child-raising with looking after aging parents. In addition to this, our birth rates are at historic lows, and many in the middle classes of wealthier countries are putting off childbirth for a decade or more. The result is a population that is getting older and one in which the number of workers who pay the taxes that we all depend upon is getting smaller.

US Population Distribution by Age Group

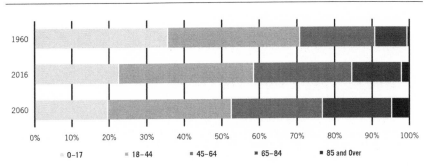

0–17   18–44   45–64   65–84   85 and Over

Source: US Census Bureau

In Japan, where this trend first manifested itself, the proportion of the population accounted for by people aged sixty-five and above has risen from 12 percent in 1990 to over 25 percent today. During the same period, the proportion aged eighteen and under has fallen from 19 percent to just over 10 percent.[48] The same trend, albeit on a less dramatic scale, is present in each of the other G7 countries. In the United States, the decline in the younger population began in the mid-1990s, while the tipping point for the increasing proportion of elderly began around 2010. This has huge implications for how we fund Social Security (the subject of a later chapter), fund health care generally, and pay for elder care for future generations. This last point is made all the more urgent and important by the exploding incidence of dementia among the older population, particularly Alzheimer's disease. This hateful condition, which steadily robs the sufferer of both cognitive and motor skills, is the sixth leading cause of death in the United States today.[49] The incidence of death from Alzheimer's more than doubled in the last fifteen years, and nearly six million people in America currently live with the disease. The cost to society in terms of

48   OECD, 2014.

49   Alzheimer's Association 2018 report.

paid-for and unpaid-for care (including lost wages by in-family caregivers) is astronomical—the Alzheimer's Association estimates $277 billion a year and rising fast.

We have a situation, then, that requires a national response. As more and more of the population require care, and as the incidence of dementia grows, there needs to be a system in place that provides a framework of security for the elderly and the afflicted without breaking the bank. At present, such a framework does not exist—long-term care is the big hole in the American health care environment. According to a recent Department of Health and Human Services report, around half of all American adults will one day require some form of residential long-term care.[50] But covering the costs of that care is a minefield that very few are prepared for. There are currently four ways of paying for extended long-term care:

1. Pay for it yourself out of accumulated savings or family wealth. With the average annual cost of residential care standing at $80,000 or more, that means you or your family have to be pretty wealthy.

2. Buy an extended long-term-care insurance policy. These, however, are highly expensive and tend to come in third or fourth place in people's priorities after health insurance, life insurance, and home/mortgage insurance.

3. Be already so poor that you qualify for Medicaid. Note that neither normal private health insurance nor Medicare covers long-term care.

4. Go through all your savings until you qualify for Medicaid. This last is the most popular, and today, Medicaid pays for 61 percent of all long-term-care residents. [51]

The problem with the Medicaid route is that over 30 percent of

50   https://longtermcare.acl.gov/the-basics/how-much-care-will-you-need.html, October 2017.
51   Kaiser Family Foundation, 2017.

Americans that have yet to retire do not have any lifetime savings at all.[52] Medicaid now gets to do the majority of the heavy lifting, something it was never designed to do. So how do we reform and rejuvenate the system such that society, families, and individuals can provide security at precisely the point when it is needed the most—when you are old and vulnerable?

In an extended comparable set of countries studied by the OECD at the beginning of this decade, there are two primary systems in place for the funding and provision of long-term care (LTC):

1. LTC is one component in the universal, single-payer health system and is paid for out of the tax pool that is designated for health care.

2. A mixed system is used, whereby means testing is used to determine how much people can pay toward their own care and the remainder is on a universal (i.e., tax-based) system.

In a couple of countries utilizing a mixed approach, public costs are shared by central government and local authorities. An example of this is the United Kingdom, where recipients are means-tested every year. As an LTC recipient, your annual/monthly/weekly income (usually from pensions) is assessed, and 95 percent of this is set aside to contribute to your care, inclusive of housing, food, medications, and nursing. The local government then chips in the rest of the cost, in turn being funded by a block grant from central government and its own tax revenues. Local authorities accredit local nursing homes (some run by charities, some by for-profit organizations) and are tasked with ensuring that there are enough rooms for the expected "traffic" in any one year. For the most part, this works well. Standards of care are generally high and are rising, and responsibility for funding the system is shared by central and local governments and individuals.

However, neither the UK nor any of the other countries surveyed

---

52 SCAN Foundation, March 2013.

(whether they be using the universal or the mixed system) can escape the oncoming train of demographic change and increasing costs in an era of shrinking workforces. At some point, tax income (both central and local) is not going to meet the needs of an increasingly older and mentally challenged population. It is here that the objections of conservatives (setting aside the panic-mongers who characterize this whole approach as "socialist") have real validity and must be taken seriously. How do you build a system in which funding will be there to take care of our grandparents, or even our parents, in their old age?

Before coming back to this question, let's throw one more piece of data into the equation. Back in the mid-twentieth century (the time for which the current system of funding health care was designed), factory jobs for life paying good wages were plentiful, workers got paid defined-benefit pensions, and life expectancy was lower. If you retired at sixty-five, chances were that your retirement would be relatively short. Today, jobs are not for life; pensions—if given at all—are "defined contribution," usually in some form of 401(k); and you are going to live ten years longer, at least. Each of these phenomena is in its own right a game changer for long-term-care funding. The one that we could control the most, however, was the issue of pensions. The movement from defined benefit to defined contribution represented one of the most significant power shifts from labor to capital seen in the last fifty years. Its effect on how people were prepared for retirement was dramatic—no longer was there a guaranteed monthly payment that was directly tied to your final salary, just a pot of money (usually much less) to be used as you saw fit. Needless to say, the pot was not always there in the later part of retirement. If defined-benefit pensions were still around today (and I understand the heart failure that gives to any CEO or CFO reading this), the burden on Medicaid of LTC financing would not be there, and families would not have to see their loved ones run through all their life savings and assets just to qualify for Medicaid.

It's this observation that leads to a potential road forward. The key to achieving individual security for old age while at the same time lessening the stress on Medicaid is clearly to build up assets for all workers for use in later life. Well, you might say, we already have that, and it's called Social Security—which is true. But what if a supplemental system were to be introduced—call it your Long-Term Care Fund—whereby the younger you are, the more you are encouraged to invest in LTC vouchers? The earlier you invest, the greater the effect of compound interest that would accrue to those vouchers and the greater the pot of money available to you if and when you needed long-term care. This being a Democratic *Libertarian* society, you would have the option to bail out of such a system at any point, at which time your funds would be frozen. You could also rejoin at any point. And if, say, at age seventy you made the determination that you were never going to need LTC, then you could withdraw funds either in total or as an annuity. Clearly, whether or not to participate in such a scheme would be an individual choice, but there would be individual consequences as well. Should you decide not to participate, then the normal rules of business would apply, and all assets would have to be exhausted before Medicaid could kick in.

As a quid pro quo to individuals stepping up more to take care of their needs in later life, a Democratic Libertarian government would also commit to a massive increase in funding for Alzheimer's and dementia research, not only to provide greater security for those afflicted but also to reduce the overall cost burden of these diseases and to free up resources for health spending elsewhere.

The conservative angel on my shoulder is whispering in my ear, "This is all well and good, Simon, but let's go back to that single-payer system you want us to adopt. Given the demographic changes you have outlined, how on earth are we going to pay for that?" To which I would reply very simply, if the US government already spends more on health care than many of its peers elsewhere spend *in total* (i.e., public and private), is it beyond the genius of Americans to work out how to do it as least as well as them?

Let's concede a few points here. This is a very large country, much larger than any of its comparable peers. That makes a single-payer system more complex to administer. (Perhaps a state-by-state single-payer system?) We seem to suffer more than other countries from injuries and deaths caused by traffic accidents and guns. (Let's deal with those problems at their source.) Dementia seems to take a bigger toll in America than elsewhere (ditto). So, maybe we can't hold spending in a single-payer system to 7 percent, as many of our competitors do. But is it really beyond us to bring it down to 10 percent? The country that landed men on the moon? Leads world technology? Invented stealth aircraft? Really?

One thing I do know is that health security is a fundamental building block to financial security. A healthy population is a productive population. And a productive population is a secure population. Health care is not a cost. It is—like its cousin, education—an investment.

All this being said, there is one final brick in the wall of physiological security (the second Maslow level), and that is social security.

The US health system is broken

We spend three times what our peer countries spend, for a worse outcome. Health security means absence of fear that ill-health will bankrupt you and put you out on the street.

Health Reform

Create a single payer system, open to all

Enable the government to negotiate drug prices

Eliminate health insurers, except for those who opt to stay in a private system

Create individual Long-Term Care funds (optional)

Increase funding for Alzheimer's and dementia research

14

Social Security or "Welfare"?

W hat exactly is "social security"? It's another of those terms that gets thrown around and, in some cases, demonized as something that "socialist societies" do. It also comes packaged as "welfare," "the welfare state," "scrounging," and "living off taxpayers." None of which sound good.

In fact, social security comes in two flavors:

1. the bedrock security that is afforded citizens when, for whatever reason, they reach rock bottom in their lives and desperately need assistance to get them back on their feet, and

2. the security that comes with being able to make fundamental decisions about your life that are social in nature and that do not naturally belong in the realm of government to decide.

The first type is literally a last resort. When financial, economic, or health security fail, social security is there to meet the most basic needs to a human being in Maslow's hierarchy—housing, food, and physical well-being. It is judgment-free, meaning that it does not take into account whether you brought this state of affairs onto your own head or whether you are blameless.

Many people of a more socially and politically puritan outlook say that it is not government's place to bail such people out, especially if it is their own fault. That's what churches and other social charities are for. Why burden the abstemious, frugal, and moral taxpayer with the cost of those who abuse alcohol or spend beyond their means or have a child out of wedlock in their teens? Yes, Christians (and many other religions) say that it is our responsibility to look after the weakest in our midst and to love our neighbors as ourselves, but that still does not mean government has to pay for those who have reached the bottom of the pile.

Leaving aside the moral argument here, however, there are excellent reasons why government should indeed intervene when things go horribly wrong for individuals or families—and that is because individual insecurity can often mushroom into societal insecurity with all the problems that can bring. I am not talking about the downfall of a nation here, or even societal collapse. I am talking about the appalling insecurity that can be brought to a neighborhood, a town, or a city—the sort of insecurity that is contagious and can lead to entire regions entering into decline. For, when a neighborhood reaches a tipping point in insecurity (for example, when a town's biggest employer closes down), a set of dominoes starts to collapse. People without employment start to run through their savings, take on debt, and eventually have to start choosing between basics such as rent, food, and health insurance. They individually become highly insecure, with all the consequences that we examined earlier.

But, most important, widespread individual insecurity then leaches into the security of the surrounding society. The local tax base is depleted; services are cut back. School budgets are slashed, with things like after-school programs the first to go, leaving latchkey kids to work out what to do in an afternoon with no money and nowhere to go. Guess who "helps them out"? Neighborhood gangs who prey on the children's need for people to hang out with and groups to belong to. Before long, latchkey kids are gang members in training and become mules for drug dealing. There are fewer police to control this, fewer firefighters, fewer health facilities, doctors, and nurses. The neighborhood falls into terminal decline, and with that comes despair and crime. This is what happened in such cities as Flint, Michigan, and Youngstown, Ohio. It's not just in the classic Midwest rust belt, either—you can find this dynamic at play as far afield as Stockton, California, and Newark, New Jersey. And once, as a city, you fall down that hole, it is incredibly difficult to get out. Decisions start to be made on a financial basis, not a human one, and that's when you get outright scandals such as the water crisis in Flint.

This is why social security is needed—to prevent societal decay from progressing to a point that is not only irretrievable but also causing other problems leading to the downward spiral happening faster and with more dreadful consequences. Because if we can stop that decay in its tracks, if we can restore even the most basic security to people who have reached the bottom, then we will save ourselves a lot of money in the long run. If we can prevent the influx of gangs and of drugs, for example, we will not have to spend so much money on privately run prisons. If we can maintain health services on at least a basic level, then we will not need to bear the costs of chronic diseases through Medicaid later on. If we can use social security money to provide retraining facilities, maybe we create a future taxpayer. Social security is an investment in people who need a second chance—and, just like any other investment, we can easily calculate its return.

Here is the final kicker: In a really well-run society, social security becomes a rare commodity, and the budget allotted to it declines over time. A society that is healthy, well educated, and prepares its population for the jobs of today in a stable, growing economy is less likely to see its people develop chronic illness, less likely to have problems of substance abuse, less likely to have a class of chronically unemployed. In short, it is far less likely to need to spend its money on the ultimate fallback of social insurance.

Beyond this traditional definition of "social security" there is another. This is the realm of decisions that individuals sometimes need to take and that are inherently private in nature, but which also spur moral debate. These include assisted suicide, the medical use of marijuana, and the ultimate divider—abortion. In each of these, an individual may want to do something that they view as critical to their own existence but of which portions of society disapprove. Usually, these portions are religious in nature and base their disapproval on the teachings of their faith. And, very often, these groups want to impose their beliefs on the population as a whole. But to do so, they have to revert to that one institution that politically they revile under any other circumstance, Big Government. Because how else can you bring about a society-wide ban on abortion than by legislating for such a ban, either through Congress or via the Supreme Court? Absent the right of a president to bring about such a rule through an executive order, there is no other way unless, of course, you resort to government at the state level.

Since the landmark ruling *Roe v. Wade* (1973) established that abortion was a constitutional right—and until such time as that ruling is overturned—the law of the United States stands in the way of abortion abolitionists. So they have turned to the legislatures of individual states to pass laws that, while not outlawing abortion per se, make it more and more difficult for providers to function and for women to procure an abortion. Such laws include rules that require licensed physicians to perform the procedure, clinics being linked to accredited hospitals, prohibition of the use of public funding, regulation of private insurance to prevent abortions being covered, state-mandated waiting periods, and mandatory counseling.[53] As a result, twenty-two states now have fewer than five abortion clinics operating within their borders, and five (North Dakota, South Dakota, Wyoming, Missouri, and Mississippi) have only one apiece.

---

53 Guttmacher Institute, 2018.

In such states, it is the poor and underprivileged that bear the brunt of these policies the most. A middle-class woman needing or wanting an abortion, for example, can buy a plane ticket to a state where clinics are still relatively plentiful and legally protected. A poor woman cannot. And so, whether you are morally for or against the ability of a woman to decide whether or not to abort her pregnancy, we still have a large societal problem: There is now an inherent inequality of the law as it is applied both between states and between socioeconomic classes. Those in restrictive states or at the bottom rungs of society do not enjoy the same level of security applied to their more liberal or richer neighbors. For them, the consequences of not being able to secure an abortion can lead to financial and economic insecurity, health insecurity, and, in the case of pregnant teens, educational insecurity.

Morally, abortion is an extremely difficult philosophical question. It rests upon whether we, as humans, have the right to end life before it has really begun; the issue of when life really does begin (at conception or at the point of sustainability?); and the rights of the mother to live her life as she best sees fit, especially if the pregnancy was the result of rape or incest; and, in extremis, whose life is more important if the pregnancy threatens the life of the mother—the fetus's or the parent's? It is not my intent to delve into these questions here, save to say that I suspect that the vast majority of people find these questions disturbing, whether they be liberal or conservative. But the question I do have to ask is: Is this any of government's business?

That government does get involved in moral issues is indisputable. And, in some cases, it has every business doing so. But the key issue here is that it does so not to take a moral stand but *to defend and uphold the security of the individual and of society as a whole.* Why does government prohibit murder or theft? It's not because Moses came down from the Mount with the Ten Commandments in hand; it's because murder and theft injure other people, deprive them of security, and endanger the security and stability of society as a whole. Does abortion do that? Those on the Religious Right would say the security of the fetus needs to be protected just as much as the security of any other person. Those on the Left would argue that the superior security here rests with the life and well-being of the mother. This is not an argument in which the government should have a dog. And, more tellingly, we should ask whether abortion actually makes society itself more insecure. It is difficult to argue that it does, when women are able to regain their own individual security and live more fulfilled lives as a consequence—and when they are not seeking abortions in back-room, illegal, and life-threatening circumstances.

Because this is such a difficult argument—and because it is more philosophical than political—many countries have resorted to allowing their legislators to vote their consciences on the issue. This means the political parties themselves do not lay down rules or litmus tests for their candidates or representatives but allow them quietly to vote on the issue in privacy. This seems to work for smaller, more homogeneous societies. For the United States, which is so vast and diverse, and which contains fifty-one governments within its borders (not counting sovereign Native American nations), this solution would probably not be as easy or effective. It certainly would not stop lobbying by religious or liberal interests or them holding candidates to their own litmus tests. One could argue that this could truly be a case where state rights trump those of the federal government in getting involved, but even there the question remains: Is this really an area in which government *should* be involved? As it stands, the myriad of ways in which states have sought to get around *Roe v. Wade* has already created inequality and insecurity. So, clearly, that is not the answer if what we are seeking is a truly democratic way of allowing people to decide on this issue without significantly damaging the security of individuals and portions of society without their input.

From a Democratic Libertarian point of view, it could be argued that this is perhaps an issue that should be devolved down to the smallest unit of government possible—the county. Health care and education are already largely dispensed at this level, so why not let the people of a smaller, defined area decide how they want to live? Voters in Wake County, North Carolina, could decide to allow for the provision of abortion services while in neighboring Johnston County, voters could decide the opposite. If the issue is really that important to an individual voter or family, they can choose the county in which they want to live with this as one criterion. Overall, however, the likelihood of widespread inequality and insecurity—while not completely solved for—would be mitigated. Even better, the issue would be taken out of the realm of big government, where it has never belonged.

In case anyone feels the need to object to such a solution, let me remind them that other similarly hot issues have been amicably resolved in such a way for a very long time. There are still to this day "dry" counties in the United States, where the purchase of alcohol is not allowed—because the citizens want to live that way. Arguably, the county should be the arbiter of any issue that has the label "moral" attached to it. Should we legalize recreational marijuana? Should we allow adult shops? Should we allow gambling? What conditions should we attach to divorce? These are all moral choices that individual communities should be empowered to make on their own through the ballot box—and that have no place whatsoever at the level of federal or state government. Governments are not arbiters of morals, except where they damage or affect the security of individuals or society as a whole. That role belongs to religions, communities, and individuals. Why else would the Amish continue to coexist so peacefully with the rest of American society—maintaining their own communities, their rules, their lives? That does not mean they can murder, rape, and pillage as they want (which they don't)—those transgressions come under the rules governing the whole of society. But where that is not the case, the rule should be "government, get out of the way."

On that rule we can then build the next building block of a healthy and functional society—a sense of "belonging."

There are two types of social security

The Social Safety Net

EXAMPLES:

State pensions
Unemployment benefits
Medicare/Medicaid
Job training
Relocation assistance
Drug rehab

PRINCIPLES:

Prevent individual collapse
to prevent societal collapse
on local, regional, and
national levels

Social Laws

EXAMPLES:

Abortion
Religious exemption
Gender identification
Anti-vaccination
Monument removal

PRINCIPLES:

Do no harm, especially to
the weakest among us

Does the government
really have any say?

If in doubt, resolve at
the most local level

PART THREE

(Re)Building a Sense of Belonging

15

What Does "Belonging" Mean?

B elonging is a desired natural state for almost all mammals on the planet. Whales belong to pods, lions to prides, wolves to packs, and humans to all sorts of different groupings. The fact that we have so many words to describe different units of belonging according to one's species attests to how ingrained this need is. Not to belong, in many species, is a one-way ticket to oblivion. The silverback gorilla, for example, once he is played out in terms of his ability to lead his troop, wanders off into the jungle to expire alone. The male lion who fails in his bid to lead his pride has to find another if he is to survive. To "belong" is part of our natural animal DNA.

To belong is to be a part of something, to be included, to survive. It is also an active state, as usually when one belongs to a group, one is also a contributor to that group in one way or another. There is a role to play, and that role not only solidifies the right to belong but also gives satisfaction and pleasure. It makes one proud to belong. But belonging to what? Usually, it is to something that is bigger than me. It is where fear (for me) is absent, and there is a feeling of well-being and joy in being a part of this something. In short, it is where I feel welcome.

In a well-functioning society—one that is based on widespread democratic values based on freedom—a government's ability to provide a framework of security in all the forms we have so far discussed sets up the conditions for society as a whole to be welcoming and for people to feel that they belong. In such a society, there is no room for "otherism" or for the ostracizing of people who are in some way "different." In a widely welcoming society, diversity is celebrated, and those who are different are accepted as contributing something to the whole. They are made to feel as if they belong. It goes without saying, therefore, that there is no room for inequality under the law or for unfairness in any form. A free and democratic society is a place where you are free to belong—and where freedom itself belongs.

In different circumstances, however, belonging—or its absence—can also lead to destruction. This can manifest itself in two ways that often interact with one another to lead to highly toxic results. To understand this better, think of belonging as a spectrum akin to that used in science to describe acidity. On one end is alkaline and on the other acid. Imagine a free, open, and democratic society—this is an alkaline state. Now imagine a society in which belonging is denied to certain groups and/or in which it is reserved only to groups designed to exclude others. That is the acid state. Belonging in this state is the preserve of the privileged or the anointed and serves as a weapon with which to render others subservient or, worse, dispensable.

We have seen this acid-like state all too often in modern history. In Nazi Germany, for example, one belonged to the Party (or, if young, to the Hitler Youth). To do so not only was a good method of survival in a brutal society but it also made many people feel in some way superior. And that was because the focal point of belonging in this case was to ensure that at least one population did *not* belong—the Jews. To not belong was dangerous and often fatal. To be a Jew was to be an "other" on whom all the ills of society could be blamed, allowing an alternative universe and an alternative truth to exist and flourish. The same was true in South Africa, where whites belonged to the privileged minority that held political and economic power, and blacks—the majority in their own country—were left on the outside, made to feel and be subservient and lacking in power. If we are honest, that is how the American South also ran its society during the era of Jim Crow.

Often, though, those who are made to feel that they do not belong—whether they be Jews, blacks, LGBTQ—find belonging in the outcast group to be an immense source of moral strength. It was this that Martin Luther King tapped into—the pride and dignity of a race that was forever on the wrong end of society, the economy, and politics. This strength and, yes, nobility gave birth to resistance just as that which Mandela channeled in South Africa prevented that society from melting into a bloodbath. Even—and perhaps especially—here, in twenty-first-century America, belonging matters.

The difference in these types of belonging is found in the second key word of Maslow's third level of his hierarchy. That word is "love." He titles this level as "Love and Belonging" and defines it as the presence of friendship, family, intimacy, and a sense of connection. Those on the Authoritarian Right who use belonging as an exclusive privilege and who excoriate and bully those outside the favored circle do so in order to sow discord and to keep "enemies" and "others" in a state of constant fear. But the politicians and statesmen who have recognized the intrinsic link between love and belonging—Ghandi, Mandela, King—have all achieved amazing things for society, and usually through nonviolent means. All of them can truthfully be described as Democratic Libertarians, inhabiting the bottom left-hand corner of our quadrant.

Yes, you may say, these were indeed all extraordinary men who achieved extraordinary things, but there are precious few of them in history. You yourself, Simon, have said that most modern governments fall into the top right-hand corner—that of the Authoritarian Right. No one exemplifies this more than the current president of the United States, who uses bullying and division as everyday levers of ruling. How, then, can society not only prevent this but actively build an environment of love and belonging? More to the point, how can government do this and make it last?

I would argue that this rests in what I call the "five equalities."

Equality in the Sight of the Law

At its very root, belonging is the ability to participate and flourish in society in the absence of fear. This means there has to be rock-solid confidence that everyone—whatever their color, creed, sexuality, or political leaning—is treated exactly the same under the law. There is a reason that Lady Justice (hailing from the Roman goddess Iustitia) is so often portrayed wearing a blindfold. She is blind as to who you are—justice will be imparted equally whether you are rich or poor, white or Native American, powerful or powerless. This idea is supposed to extend beyond the courts right back to the making of the laws that the courts enforce. Legislatures, as the writers of the law, are supposed to bring forth legislation that neither favors nor penalizes any particular group—although, as we would all cynically point out, this has rarely (if ever) been the case. Just as the making and administration of the law are both supposed to apply equally to everybody, so is the application and protection of the law in our everyday lives. The police, in whatever guise we might find them (local, county, FBI) are supposed to apply the law equally and without bias wherever they go.

Right now, equality in the sight of the law is a cruel joke for some Americans. For far too many, the ability to live their lives quietly and without interference—to truly belong to a wider society—is but a pipe dream. If you are a young African-American male, your chances of living in the absence of fear in vast chunks of America are pretty much zero. This is not just due to the tendency in many American police forces to racially profile their suspects (sometimes unwittingly and sometimes, as in Arizona under Sheriff Arpaio, very deliberately), it is about the laws that not only allow them to do so but actively promote it.

Take, for example, the "war on drugs" and how the laws promoting that war treated the possession of cocaine. In 1986, Congress passed the Anti-Drug Abuse Act, which, among other things, established a difference between the possession of crack cocaine and powder cocaine. Under the mistaken belief that the former was more damaging than the latter, the act imposed a ratio in sentencing for the crime of possession that proved to be disastrous for one population in particular—African-Americans. Under the act, the same sentence was made mandatory for the possession of a certain amount of crack cocaine as was the case for one hundred times that amount of powder cocaine. So, if you had five grams of crack, you would receive the same sentence as someone who was found in possession of five hundred grams of powder. This was known as the 100:1 rule. Since crack was cheaper, the law ensnared many more African-Americans than other races. As an example, in 2009, of the 5,669 crack offenders sentenced, 79 percent were black, 10 percent white, and 10 percent Hispanic. The figures for possession of powder cocaine (which, remember, required more than one hundred times the possession of crack) were diametrically opposite—28 percent black, 17 percent white, and 53 percent Hispanic.[54] As a result, far more African-Americans went to jail for cocaine than any other race, leaving broken families and shattered dreams behind them. Even though, in 2010, Congress and the Obama administration severely reformed this law (bringing the ratio down from 100:1 to a still unsatisfactory 18:1), the die was cast. African-American males became fair game in both law enforcement and the judicial system and, even worse, among wannabe law enforcement.

When Trayvon Martin was killed by a local vigilante in Florida in 2012, the feeling that African-American males had become an endangered species was eloquently expressed by President Obama, who said:

---

54   US Sentencing Commission, 2010.

There are very few African-American men in this country who haven't had the experience of being followed when they were shopping in a department store. That includes me. There are very few African-American men who haven't had the experience of walking across the street and hearing the locks click on the doors of cars. That happens to me—at least before I was a senator. There are very few African-Americans who haven't had the experience of getting on an elevator and a woman clutching her purse nervously and holding her breath until she had a chance to get off. That happens often.

This was the first black president of the United States talking about his own personal experience of *not* belonging in a society in which he was supposed to belong. An entire section of American society now lives in fear because of who they are. In state after state, the "crime" of driving while black (DWB), for example, has become endemic. These are people who are made to feel they do not belong. And that has major consequences. If you can't belong in society as a whole, where can you belong? In gangs, that's where. Gangs are all about belonging—you get to belong by proving yourself, whether it is by doing a drug deal or committing a random drive-by shooting. And once you belong, you are protected, your family is protected, and you feel safe, even as you pursue a life of crime.

As Maslow would perhaps point out, were he around to do so, what is missing here is love. Yes, the black male may love his family—he may even love his fellow gang members—but the critical point is that society does not love him. And why should they? He's a thug, a criminal, a drug dealer, perhaps even a murderer. But how did he get here? Because the law was written against him and is applied unequally against him. Because there was no equality in the sight of the law when it was first written, this section of society was essentially written off. America was saying to the young African-American male, "We don't value you, we don't love you, you are not part of us—you don't belong."

Such a message is devastating at both a societal and an individual level and certainly does not lead to security on either level. What we have done to African-Americans, we also have done over the ages to entire populations that have emigrated to the United States. We have done it to Jews, Germans, Italians, Irish, Chinese, Japanese, and Latin Americans. For a country that has thrived on immigration—and, indeed, embodies the entire ethos of growth through immigration and diversity—we have an ugly history of trying to make these people feel as if they do not belong.

Even today, white supremacists fret about the "browning" of America and hark back to old prejudices against assimilated groups. One only had to watch the ugly scenes at Charlottesville where white thugs bearing torches marched through the streets chanting "Jews will not replace us" to realize that there is in America today an increase in populist fascism that thrives on "otherism"—the need to make others feel they do not belong. What is far worse is that this is being fostered and encouraged by our own government and our own president as a means of political survival—play to your base, "divide and thrive," and you might just get elected again. Bugger the fact that your own wife and in-laws are immigrants and that your own family emigrated from Germany! To tell the truth, I would have far more sympathy if the people in the streets of Charlottesville had been Native Americans. They above all have lost far more to white immigration than anybody else— and they, more than anyone else, feel that they no longer belong in the land that was once theirs.

The present government, eager to play to its base of the disenfranchised, has sought to make immigration of any sort the primary focus of "otherism" in politics today. Immigration has become the meme that expresses all frustration. Not satisfied with focusing on illegal immigration and building a wall, the government is now severely restricting legal immigration as well, reducing the numbers of green cards and visas available to those wanting to come legally to live here. The irony of this is not lost on those employers who depend most on foreign-born workers to allow them to thrive and dominate in their research and development, engineering, and business growth. Just talk to all the giants of Silicon Valley, where Indians, Chinese, and all other types of Asians are helping power America's most successful industries and companies. Or, to go much further down the technology chain, talk to the lettuce farmers of Yuma, Arizona, who depend on Mexican workers to bring in the harvest. In reducing the opportunities for such workers to come here, the administration is choking off future growth and handing the market over to those whom it deems our enemies—for example, the Chinese.

The even deeper irony here is that we educate huge numbers of these data analysts, engineers, and software developers here in our own universities. Once we have imparted to them all they need to know to be successful in their chosen careers, should we not be doing everything in our power to keep them, to make them feel like they belong? Instead, the administration is restricting their ability to stay and sending them back to their countries to compete with us from there! As a colleague of mine once famously said about a competitor, "We knew they could shoot themselves in the foot. We just didn't know they could reload so fast." When you make sure that whole populations feel unwelcome, especially in a country such as ours, you qualify as a serial foot-shooter.

But what of illegal immigrants, a subject that is used as a lightning rod in our political discourse? Let's start off with a few (inconvenient) facts:

1. The number of illegal immigrants living in the United States has been actually declining over the last decade and now stands at 10.5 million souls.[55]

2. The vast majority of those have been in the country for over a decade. As of 2017, only 20 percent of the adults here illegally had entered in the previous five years.

3. The number of apprehensions at the Southwest border declined by 76

---

55   Pew Research Center, June 2019.

percent between 2000 and 2018.[56] Between 1983 and 2001, annual illegal crossings over the Southwest border ranged between 1 million and 1.65 million. Today, they range between 300,000 and 400,000.

4. As of 2016, 44 percent of long-term illegal immigrants were actually visa overstays—and 65 percent of net arrivals from 2008 to 2015 were also overstays. [57]

The takeaway is that the illegal immigration "problem" is not a current problem; it is an inherited one, and the role of the Southwestern border pales in significance compared to the number of visa overstays. This casts a dubious light on the current administration's focus on building a wall. Indeed, the wall is more of a metaphor aimed at casting blame for imagined wrongs (rape, crime, job substitution) on a brown "other." It is aimed at making whites feel they are the true "belongers" while making immigrants feel as if they will never belong. This policy was well known in Arizona for many years, where the infamous Maricopa County sheriff, Joe Arpaio, made it his life's work to harass Mexicans in the state by profiling them in traffic stops and then trying to assess their immigration status. The ultimate result was that Hispanics in the area would not cooperate with the police and that crime in their neighborhoods, mostly gang-related, mushroomed. Arpaio was ordered by the Department of Justice to cease racial profiling, failed to do so, was prosecuted, and then, before a sentence could be passed, was pardoned by Donald Trump. There could be no clearer message to the Hispanic population in this country that they were not considered as belonging—indeed, that they would be hunted down and deported.

The same message was sent with brutal clarity when the Justice Department announced a policy of separating children from their parents at the border. More than 2,000 children had been forcibly removed from their

---

56   US Customs and Border Protection, 2019.
57   Center for Migration Studies.

parents before national outrage forced the government to backtrack, although attempts to reunite the families failed in the majority of cases. The nation was treated to television pictures and newspaper reports of kids kept weeping in cages—something that no civilized nation had done in over seventy years. The entire message that the government wanted to send (broadcasting it to its exclusionist base) was "you are not welcome here, you do not belong."

The problem with this—aside from human rights violations that could land the United States in the International Criminal Court—is that it sends the same message to Hispanics and immigrants of all origins right across the country. In doing so, it creates an atmosphere of insecurity that is both personal and societal. But in "otherizing" illegal (and legal) immigrants, the administration and its supporters are deliberately ignoring two important facts: (a) that the problem is no longer with the border or with the influx of immigrants as a whole and (b) that the eleven million are already here. They exist. They are part of our society. They pay taxes and make Social Security payments, even though they will never see a payout from Social Security. They are among us. They mow our lawns, pick our vegetables, wash our cars, provide us with great places to eat. They participate on our PTAs, give to charity, and contribute to our art and literature. They are here. However much the Right might want it, to deport all eleven million would not only be impossible, but would deprive the economy and society as a whole of a population that actually fuels growth. All they want in return is to belong.

But how can this be achieved once the issue has become so politicized and used to ensure the continuance of division? Luckily, there is considerable precedence for this in the United States—ultimately, the Jews, Italians, Germans, Greeks, Norwegians, Swedish, Chinese, Japanese, and Amish all came to feel they belonged and could confidently start to call themselves Americans. The same will eventually occur with Hispanics, Arabs, and Africans. But it will need a nudge from the political system. First of all, politicians must openly recognize that immigrants to the United States are behaving logically, both cognitively and emotionally: They are looking for that thing we all need as the basis of our lives—*security*. If they do that, legislators and others can stop the demonization of people whose only desire is for themselves and their children to live in peace and make a living.

To do this, we all need to come to terms with the fact that the eleven million are here. They exist. Now that they are here, how do we deal with them, and how do we lessen the chances that people will need to come here to escape the violence and misery of their homelands while setting out a logical and practical path to legitimate immigration? Where the eleven million are concerned, we need to understand and acknowledge the fact that they do, for the vast part, contribute to the economy, pay taxes, and help fill the Social Security pot. If that is so, then in return, there should be a calm and logical path to citizenship that does not involve outlandish requirements such as returning to their homelands. Examples of these could include the following:

· If you and your family have been here for ten years or more, have not been convicted of a felony, have been either in full-time education or employment, and have paid taxes, then you automatically qualify for a green card. From there on in, the rules for transitioning from green card to full citizenship apply.

· If you and/or your family have been in the country for less than ten years, are in full-time education and/or have a full-time job, you can apply for a temporary student or worker's permit. Absent criminal convictions, once you have been in the country ten years, you can follow the green card route.

· If you were brought here illegally as a child, you automatically qualify for DACA status, which should lead to citizenship after five years.

· If you are granted asylum for any of the reasons under the law why asylum is appropriate, you may stay, work, and study in the country and pursue a path to citizenship over time. (In this instance, only Congress could decide what circumstances should be considered as valid for the granting of asylum, so as to preempt capricious administrations from changing those rules to meet their political needs, as is happening now.)

Of course, exclusions should apply, just as they do for green card holders. If you are convicted of a felony, the game is over, and you get deported once you have served your sentence. If you have avoided paying taxes, you have six months to pay what you owe, or you return to your country of origin.

In all of this, one overarching principle applies: The eleven million who are already here are accorded equality in the sight of the law. This does not mean there would not be laws that solely applied to them. Of course there would be. But they would be applied with the same evenness and fairness that we strive to apply to justice everywhere in the system.

The second pillar of any system seeking to reduce illegal immigration would be to mitigate the reasons why such immigration exists in the first place. Today, if we are looking at Hispanic immigration, the primary sources of immigrants are Honduras, Guatemala, and other hot spots in Central America. Soon, we may expect a spike in Venezuelans as they make their way from Colombia up to our borders. Why do these people come? Because they live in violent societies where the rule of law is either non-existent or completely corrupt; societies in which gangs recruit children, rape their mothers, and kill their fathers; societies in which the economy has completely collapsed and it is next to impossible to make a living. Unless the United States actively intervenes politically or economically to mitigate such conditions, the immigrants will keep on coming, and, yes, hundreds of thousands of them will be children. It is no accident that actual immigration from Mexico itself has significantly declined since the implementation of NAFTA (current renegotiations notwithstanding). The resultant growth of the Mexican economy and its increased interdependence with that of the United States lessened the need to immigrate. Similar investment in both the security and economies of Central America could do much to reverse their immigration trends as well—yet we treat them as minor irritants on the edges of our existence.

Finally, the path to legal immigration should be made clear, attainable, and uncomplicated. The current system is complex in the extreme, subject to manipulation for political purposes, and in places, downright comic. Consider the question (and I paraphrase): "Were you ever, have you ever been, or are you now a member of the Nazi Government of Germany?" Well, yes, I am a hundred years old and only now thinking of becoming a US citizen, and, yes, I am going to answer this question truthfully! This, and similarly ridiculous questions, are still part of the process, and we are supposed to take it seriously?

A clear and logical path to legal immigration would identify and quantify the spaces where immigration would be beneficial to the country—be that economically, socially, artistically, or for reasons of empathy and downright humanitarian decency. It would then create the opportunity for people to fill those spaces with the minimum of bureaucracy and fuss but with the appropriate amount of back-checking to ensure that we are doing this safely.

An example of where and how this could work to everyone's advantage lies in Silicon Valley. One area that seriously worries the software and technology industries is the difficulty of recruiting and hanging on to qualified data scientists and engineers. We allow tens of thousands of young people to come here from Asia to be trained in these disciplines and yet then make it difficult for them to stay in the country and contribute to our economy. The stifling bureaucracy and red tape of immigrating to this country needs to be swept aside and replaced by a system that is transparent, easy to follow, and does not break the bank of the individuals attempting to come into the country to help it compete and succeed.

None of this is especially Democratic Libertarian; it is just pure common sense. And often that is precisely what Democratic Libertarianism is—common sense. All of it, however, is focused on one thing—bringing a sense of belonging to those who are either in the country already or to those who would like to come here legally. In creating this sense of belonging—which starts as belonging in the sight of the law—we must also banish the politics of creating "unbelonging" or using narrow definitions of belonging to sow hatred and division. Only then can all the other building blocks of true belonging—belonging to society as a whole—begin to be put back into place.

Equality in Voting

The United States Constitution laid down the foundations for a republican democracy. At the time, it was advanced, given that it gave the vote equally to those sections of the population that were deemed appropriate to be trusted with such a sacred duty. In 1789, that meant land-owning white males. Since then, we have advanced that concept to include all citizens of whatever gender, race, or income bracket over the age of eighteen. We still have oddities, such as the electoral college, which has probably outlived its usefulness, but we will come back to this a little later. The overwhelming concept today is that to vote is to belong and that to belong is to vote.

Sadly, American history and the reality even of today is one of different political factions trying desperately to subvert this concept and to prevent one or both of two things: (1) the ability to vote and (2) the equivalence of each vote. During the Jim Crow era, Southern states tried everything in their power to suppress the black vote, from literacy tests to outright violence and intimidation. In one infamous example, that suppression led to a coup d'etat in one American city—Wilmington, North Carolina. On November 10, 1898, just two days after a majority-black Republican government had been elected in the city, a mob of white supremacist Democrats burned down the offices of the *Daily Record*, a black-owned newspaper. They then went on to drive out all blacks from the city, killing over sixty in the process, and to install a nonelected white Democrat government. It was and remains the only such coup in American history. (Remember, at the time, Democrats were conservative white supremacists, and Republicans—the party of

Lincoln—were "radicals." This situation would not change until the 1960s, when a Democrat president and Congress passed the Civil Rights Act, leading LBJ to famously declare, "We have lost the South.") The amazing thing is that, for the next hundred years, the history of this act of white insurrection would be taught in schools as a racially inflammatory black riot, with the new white government restoring law and order.

The sad thing is that such incidents, if less blatant and violent, still persist today. In the same state of North Carolina, a supermajority legislature was fashioned through the time-honored mechanism of gerrymandering that resulted in a Senate majority for Republicans of 10:3. One Republican legislator famously admitted that 10:3 was the final result because they could not work out how to get to 11:2. Simultaneously, the Republican legislature sought to pass voter-ID laws that a federal court later threw out, saying they were drawn up with "surgical precision" to prevent black voting. Other measures, either attempted or passed, included restrictions on Sunday voting (it being well known that black churches ran "souls to the polls" transportation for poorer black voters after church on Sunday), restrictions on early voting, and other wonderful ideas for constraining the ability of blacks (who tend to cast their ballot Democrat) to vote. And it's not just North Carolina (even though that state has the dubious distinction of being rated the least democratic—small *d*—state in the Union). Such shenanigans can be found all across the country, from Texas to Maine, Louisiana to Wisconsin. After the record turnout in the 2008 election, thirty states introduced voter-suppression legislation, and in sixteen of those the bills passed into law.[58]

When you can't vote or your vote doesn't count, you do not belong. If your vote does not mean anything, then you are not a full-fledged member of society. In saying this, I am not including people who live in states where there are built-in majorities of one party over the other—for example, New York, California, or the Dakotas. If you consciously decide to live in these

---

58   aclu.org, 2018.

places, all you can do is to fight to change attitudes and voting preferences over time. I am talking about states that deliberately suppress the vote in order to favor the ruling party's position. By indulging in these ruses (which are almost always couched in language that suggests either massive voter fraud or the necessity to protect "commonly held values"), politicians deny the right to belong to vast communities within their jurisdiction. And, in doing so, they undermine society as a whole.

How would this be dealt with in a Democratic Libertarian society? Unfortunately, if we are dealing with an issue of "equality" across the whole nation, this is not something we can leave to states' rights. If we did, we would have to acknowledge that we were living in a loose federation of sovereign states in which the definition of "voting" would have different meanings. That's not what the Constitution calls for. In this instance, both for federal and local elections, central government has to lay down one framework for all. Such a framework could involve the following:

- Electoral maps would be drawn by academic institutions according to laws laid down by Congress; local legislatures would no longer be able to draw their own maps.

- Electoral laws would include rules and regulations about the size (population) and shape of districts, without reference to party strength, ethnicity, or homogeneity.

- Federal rules governing means of voting, early voting periods, voting days, siting of polling stations, and necessary ID would be passed and applied throughout the Union.

- Voter intimidation of any type would be outlawed and punishable by law.

Finally, let us return to the issue of the electoral college. The intent of the Founders—in an era of thirteen colonies, many of which were Southern and rural and needed coaxing into the Union—was to ensure that the less densely populated states would still have a more equal say in the election of their chief executive when compared to their more urban neighbors to the North. This was also the intent of ensuring that the Senate had two seats for each state, to counterbalance the population-based composition of the House. The Senate rule has for the most part worked well, ensuring that less-populated states really do have a say in government. It is arguable, however, that the electoral college has worked as well.

In five elections in the Union's history—those of John Quincy Adams in 1824, Rutherford Hayes (1876), Benjamin Harrison (1888), George W. Bush (2000), and Donald Trump (2016)—the final electoral college vote overturned the popular vote. Trump lost the popular count by 2.8 million votes and yet secured a healthy majority in the college. It is estimated, however, that a mere 70,000 votes in key states actually tipped him over the top. Many would blame Hillary Clinton for ignoring those states. But others, this author included, would say the popular vote should have had the upper hand.

It is one thing to balance the legislature to protect the rights of less-populated states but quite another to overturn the will of the nation in the election of a chief executive who will, ultimately, have the job of representing them all. What might have worked for thirteen colonies and the need to get them all into a fledgling nation does not necessarily work in a sprawling continent of fifty states.

In a Democratic Libertarian future state, the electoral college should be deprived of its ability to thwart the will of the people and be abolished.

Equality of Opportunity

It's difficult to feel you belong if you either don't or perceive you don't have the same opportunities as everyone else to succeed. Nowhere is this more visible than in higher education, where arguments rage about whether or not positive discrimination in favor of one group or another to right previous or current wrongs and imbalances is good or poor policy. One thing is for sure, however: Equal access to both health and education is, as we have seen, fundamental to personal and societal security. And therefore, that same equality of access must be central to a feeling of belonging to the wider whole that is the nation of the United States of America. If I, as a resident (whether child or adult) of a rural neighborhood in the South, for example, do not get the same access to quality educational resources as someone living in Atlanta, Dallas, or New York, I am not going to feel as if I belong in the same society as they do.

The same thing applies in the cities. If I am someone raised and educated in the projects, I will not have the same opportunities as those going to private or high-end local schools. As a result, unless I am really single-minded about getting into a top university and proving myself as being "worthy," I am not going to feel as if I belong in a world that affords me the same opportunity as others to become a surgeon, an educator, or an entrepreneur. Obviously, such single-minded people do exist, as Ben Carson (Secretary of Housing and Urban Development and famed surgeon) constantly reminds us. However, they are exceptions to the rule. The problem then becomes "where do I belong?" And that's where gangs come in.

The promise of gang membership can either be seductive or it can be a matter of sheer survival—sometimes both. Prove yourself to be worthy of membership, goes the recruitment spiel, and we will protect you and your family. We will be your brothers. Nobody will be able to hurt you. *You will belong.* It is for this reason, if for no other, that the policies and approaches we discussed earlier relating to education, health, and justice are so important.

Equality of opportunity goes beyond where you grew up and the resources available to you. It also talks to the unspoken biases that exist in trying to find a job. As a society, we like to think we are moving beyond the racism of yesteryear and that most of us are free of the prejudices of old. In many ways, that is true. Younger generations in particular are far more likely to be blind to the ethnicity, origin, or sexual preferences of the people they intermingle with. But at the same time, prejudices continue to live under the surface and, when given permission, erupt to the surface, as happened in 2017 in Charlottesville.

White supremacy, however, is only the tip of an iceberg—the iceberg of lingering prejudicial biases that are at play just under the surface in almost all of us. In 2004, the *American Economic Review* published a study in which they had sent out résumés to companies with the names of applicants randomly assigned white-sounding names (Emily, Greg) or black-sounding names (Lakisha, Jamal).[59] Applicants with white names received 50 percent more callbacks for interviews than did their black-sounding counterparts. I will guarantee you that the people making these decisions were doing so completely unconscious of the bias they were exhibiting—they likely would not have known they had any such bias. But, replacing for a moment the fact that these were randomly assigned names with the assumption that they were real people, you can be sure the black applicants would be aware, even if only subliminally, that their mountain was the harder to climb. That does not make you feel as if you belong.

What could a Democratic Libertarian government do to mitigate such biases and such hurdles? Directly, very little. But indirectly, ensuring equal access to quality, funded education and to health care for all would start to reduce the problem, while the promotion of subliminal bias training in both government and the private sector (such as that recently undertaken by Starbucks) would at least raise awareness of the issue.

Belonging is not an easy issue for government to address head-on, but government can create the conditions whereby belonging becomes easier.

Equality of Treatment

Equal treatment is what both the Obama administration and the Supreme Court recognized when same-sex marriage was finally legalized in 2015.

---

59   American Economic Association, 2004.

They removed barriers and created conditions in which people of the same sex who wanted the same protections in relationships as marriage afforded heterosexuals could have them and feel as if they belonged in the same society as the majority.

How people are treated makes an enormous difference to the feeling of belonging. If you don't believe me, ask 50 percent of the population of the United States: women. Members of the female sex have contributed to the success of this nation since its earliest days and yet have been made to feel like second-class citizens for the vast majority of that time. It was women who sustained families in the worst possible conditions as the nation pushed west. It was women who filled the factory jobs vacated by men gone to fight in World War II. It was women who built and then delivered the aircraft that those men needed. It was women who wrangled the math necessary to get us into space and onto the moon. It was a woman who refused to give up her seat on the bus. There is no doubt that females have come a long way in the interim—there are more females in senior management and academic positions, women in the front lines of the armed forces, and a record number of successful female candidates for Congress and other governmental offices than ever before. But this has not come about due to the generosity of men. Women have had to fight every single inch of the way, starting with the Suffragette movement of the early twentieth century that secured them the vote.

And yet we still are confronted, in 2019, with the widespread mistreatment of women. The difference in pay scales for the same job is well documented—a problem that has been highlighted for decades and yet still persists. Depending on whom you listen to (the Census Bureau or the Bureau of Labor Statistics), women earn between 76 percent and 82 percent of what men do in equivalent jobs. Even if you torture the data as much as you can to adjust for things such as pregnancy, child-rearing, or choice of college degree, you still come out with a persistent gap of between 6 percent and 8 percent. Never mind why this unconscious bias exists; there is a very simple answer as to how to eliminate it: Make it visible, measure it regularly, and make management accountable. As a CEO, I would never have countenanced paying a woman less than a man for the same job. Why? Because it was easily measurable and because the CEOs who reported to me (many of whom were women) would never have let me forget it! And also, because it was the right thing to do. As of April 2018, companies in the UK are required by law to publish the gender pay gap for all jobs in a number of different ways—median, mean, quartiles, and for both salaries and bonuses. As you might imagine, a number of firms reporting their first numbers attempted to fudge them to minimize the gaps in their organizations. The press discovered these and were merciless, holding the companies' feet to the fire to do the right thing.

As this example shows, government can affect how we treat each other—and, in turn, the degree to which we feel we belong—through some fairly simple measures. Legislation is at the top of the pile here. Whether it is minorities, certain communities, or a segment as large as the number of women in society, government can lay down laws that ensure and/or promote equality of treatment. That's what the Civil Rights Act did and what the Supreme Court did for same-sex marriage. As the latter showed, if the legislature will not lead the way, perhaps the judiciary will.

In the end, it comes down not only to common sense but also to common decency. It is common sense that if people feel they belong, they will be more productive, less likely to seek alternative solutions (e.g., gangs), and more likely to treat their fellow human beings as equals. As for decency, there is, at base, a set of morals that govern how we treat each other on this earth—morals that do not depend on what religion you belong to but on basic human rules without which the human race cannot continue to exist. That being said, it is no coincidence that these same rules appear in pretty much all religions and that, in Christianity, they boil down to Jesus's admonition to "love your neighbor as yourself."

This perhaps is the very foundation of Democratic Libertarianism. It is the belief (or philosophy, if you wish) that humans are indeed created equal, that they should be treated equally, and that those who govern them do so by consent rather than by favoring one group over another. Sound familiar? Democratic Libertarianism lies at the very heart of the American Constitution that deliberately shared power among the three branches of government so that no one faction could enrich itself at the expense of others. Recognizing the fallibility of human beings (and especially those in positions of power), it limited the ability of groupings to gain power through the promise of riches to a small selectorate. In the years since 1789, the selectorate has been deliberately widened to include all facets of society, even at the cost of blood and political power. And at its base is the belief in guaranteeing certain rights that deliver security and the ability for all citizens to feel they belong. In short, Democratic Libertarianism is the one sure way of reclaiming our Constitution for all Americans.

Equality of Rights

And so, this is where we return to our roots—the rights inherent in the Founding Fathers' principles, perhaps updated a little to reflect modern society. In a Democratic Libertarian America, these would include the right to free speech and assembly, freedom of religion, equal access to justice, equal treatment under the law no matter who you are, the right to physical security, and the right to be educated and healthy.

While all of these are rooted in the common decency of the original Constitution, they also are based in common sense. Without these rights, a society ceases to have a common purpose; the society turns in on itself, favors certain groups over others, and promotes conflict. In such conditions, that society ceases to grow; it becomes less safe and more prone to find an outlet for its tensions in war.

The key to Democratic Libertarianism is that government ensures these rights continue to be enshrined in law, and then it steps out of the way to allow people to live their lives as they wish—all as long as they do not trample on the rights of others and perform the obligations expected of them. That means the government must also robustly defend these rights wherever they are threatened. Going back to Charlottesville, for example, government had the duty to pursue all of those who publicly and violently sought to deny rights to others. Luckily, because of the investment of power in all three of the branches of government, law enforcement (after the fact) did exactly that. But the executive branch, in the persona of the president, did not. In seeking false equivalence between the white supremacists and those who opposed them, Donald Trump gave permission to those who do not believe in constitutional rights for all and further indulged in the "otherism" that brought him to power in the first place. Indeed, if Democratic Libertarianism is about doing "what is right," the Trump administration and its surrogates in local legislatures all around the country appear to have focused at every turn on doing "what is wrong." They have tried to turn people against each other, tried to convince various populations that they do not belong, attacked the press and freedom of speech, attempted to reduce the overall selectorate through vote suppression, and denigrated the judiciary. How did we get here?

The sad fact is that the political systems that have been in place in the West since the end of the Second World War—and which promised so much—have started to fail. What has been variously described as "enlightened liberalism" and the "liberal order" has not delivered. As Jan Zielonka, professor of European politics at the University of Oxford, has pointed out, liberal ideals have failed to deliver consistently over the past decade, giving rise to populism not only in America but across Europe as well.[60] He alludes to how changes in governments through elections have just brought about the same policies under different labels. Those policies have led to inequality

---

60   *Inspires,* 2018 annual edition, University of Oxford Department of Politics and International Relations

within countries and between countries, with those being disadvantaged feeling that they no longer belonged and, worse, were no longer being heard. As a result, populist politicians across the EU, from Britain to Hungary, and in the United States have been able to gain power, or influence policies, that emphasize the "other" and spread the fear of "not belonging" across the Western world.

My take on this failure is that those "liberal" governments differed so little from one another and offered so little to the disadvantaged in the face of massive change that they were, in effect, interchangeable. What's more, they were all concentrated in one quadrant of the political spectrum—the Authoritarian Right. Even Clinton, Obama, and Blair, authors of a "Third Way," continued to pursue a top-down form of government that did too little to prevent the concentration of wealth in the hands of the few. Capital continued to dominate, labor was underrepresented at the seat of power, and the response to government deficits was to reduce support of the poor. Changes in the industrial landscape went unaddressed, and their consequences created the "new poor," who suddenly felt abandoned. They felt as if they no longer belonged. When you feel you no longer belong and that your government is no longer listening to you, you look elsewhere. And there, very conveniently, is the populist, eager to trade on your hurt and your fears and to turn you against your fellow citizens—all so that the populist himself can gain and hold on to power.

Belonging has to come back to the center of politics. To do so, it needs a new political system and philosophy—and that is Democratic Libertarianism.

16

Belonging and the Constitution

What the Constitution and Bill of Rights Get Right

Democratic Libertarianism, as it applies to the United States, is rooted firmly in the Constitution. Borrowing from English law (the Magna Carta) and practice (the prominence of Parliament in lawmaking), as well as from Rome (the concept of the republic), it mixed precedent with the idealism of the founding colonies and their reasons for being. Foremost among these was the *separation of church and state*. While this has been a hot topic ever since (and misinterpreted time and time again), this provision guaranteed two things:

1. The freedom to worship (or not) as you pleased

2. A prohibition on the establishment of a state-sponsored religion or church

These were not principles derived from the first colony in Virginia, as that was very much an Anglican-controlled society from the get-go. Rather, it came from the New England colonies established by Puritans fleeing persecution in England and what they perceived as a monarchy that was sliding dangerously back into Catholicism. Whether that was true or not, what was undeniable was that the king was head of the Church and that there was only one Church. Dissenters were not to be tolerated. (Ultimately this led to civil war and victory for the Puritans, even if that victory only lasted for a couple of decades.) Later, the colonies of New Jersey, Pennsylvania, and Maryland would follow suit, although in a slightly different direction. While New England followed a particular path of Protestantism, these later colonies firmly established the idea that people could worship as they wished. It was this heady idea—which so deviated from the norm in Europe—that would be embedded in the Constitution of the United States of America. Whether you were Catholic, Protestant, Mennonite, Huguenot, or Jewish, it did not matter. The decision was yours to make, and the state would never take that decision away from you. Whoever you were, and however you prayed, you still belonged.

Today, this element of the Constitution is more important than ever and is more under attack than has been the case for many years. The thin end of the wedge was laid down in 1956 when Congress and President Eisenhower adopted the phrase "In God We Trust" as the national motto and mandated that it appear on all United States currency. Up until that time, the national motto had been *E pluribus unum*—out of many, one—which had been on the Great Seal of the United States since 1782. Defenders of the new motto claimed (and still claim) that it does not violate the First Amendment, as it does not challenge the equality with which all religious establishments are treated. There is some merit in this argument inasmuch as the use of the phrase does not establish a state religion, nor does it prohibit the establishment of a religion by others. However, in a society in which new religions are being introduced into the country on a continual basis through immigration—and in some of which (such as Hinduism) there are multiple gods—it implies a monotheism that is at odds with these other beliefs. As such, adherents to these religions may feel as if they belong less than do adherents to the Abrahamic faiths. Not to mention that increasing numbers of Americans belong to no particular faith at all.

Between 2007 and 2014, those believing in God with certainty in the US fell from 71 percent to 63 percent.[61] Those not believing at all rose from 5 percent to 9 percent (still a relatively low percentage compared to other developed countries). Among those who declared a religious affiliation (i.e., excluding atheists or the nonaffiliated), the groups most likely to declare that they do not believe in God included Buddhists, Hindus, and, interestingly, Jews. For these people as well as out-and-out atheists, the motto "In God We Trust" has a hollow ring. I hear you say, so what? Just because this minority does not believe in God does not mean that we should abandon our overall national trust in the Deity. America was founded as a Christian nation. John Fea, a scholar at Messiah University, wrote perhaps the most defining treatise on whether or not this was true and finds the question to be highly nuanced.[62] For example, the Constitution does not actually refer to any deity at all, but the constitutions of many of the states joining the Union did—and it was a Christian deity. Not all the Founders were Christians—indeed, Jefferson excised any reference to Jesus as a deity out of his own personal Bible. And yet, most of the people of that era would likely have affirmed the new republic to be a Christian nation.

The problem for today is that the most avowedly Christian groups— broadly termed "Evangelicals"—have adopted a political stance that not only challenges Jefferson's "wall" between church and state but subverts core Christian teaching to political ends, such as having a conservative Supreme Court, banning abortion outright and teaching Christian values above all others in our schools. In other words, they want their Christian values (note the word "their") to be translated by government into law. They want

---

61   Pew Research Center, Religious Landscape Study.
62   John Fea. *Was America Founded as a Christian Nation?* (Louisville, Ky.: Westminster John Knox Press, 2011).

government to institutionalize their moral values over all others and enforce them by secular law. As a set of beliefs, that is almost the purest demonstration of the Authoritarian Right—we know what is best for you, we will enshrine it in law, and we will punish you if you transgress. There is very little room between this and the idea of Sharia Law in Islamic states. (Ironically, extreme Evangelicals use Sharia Law as a bogeyman to push for their own enshrinement of Christian mores into American law.)

In a Democratic Libertarian society, this is anathema. In this environment, government is there to bring a framework of safety that is designed to foster a feeling of belonging. Government is not there to dictate what I believe or how I practice my beliefs; the only time it can do so is if such practice endangers the safety of society or individuals, which is why cults are so carefully monitored. Other than that, the duty of government is to create a framework in which beliefs can be held and practiced and then *step out of the way*. As such, a Democratic Libertarian government would protect the liberty of all religions, as well as those who have no religion at all.

In the end, my own beliefs fall squarely with those of Abraham Lincoln, who, when asked if he would join any particular church, replied that he would do so with one that inscribed above its altar the injunction of Jesus to "love the Lord thy God with all thy heart, with all thy soul, and with all thy mind, and to love thy neighbor as thyself."[63] That at least has at its heart the concept of all "neighbors" belonging.

To belong in its widest sense means to be able to live your life not only in the absence of fear but also in the knowledge that you can contribute without fear of negative consequences. In too much of the world today, the ability to do this is noticeable by its absence. Perhaps the poster boy for such repression is modern-day Russia. To oppose the government today in Russia is to invite prosecution under a deeply flawed legal system, imprisonment, and death (whether in prison or not). This applies even when you have

---

63   Grant N. Havers. *Lincoln and the Politics of Christian Love* (University of Missouri, 2009).

"retired" from being active against the government, as the Novichok attack on an ex-Russian spy in the United Kingdom amply demonstrates. Indeed, he was not the only one. There have been at least fourteen such attacks in the United Kingdom by Russian operatives over the last decade alone.

Most of the developed world holds *freedom of expression and assembly* close to the heart of its political system. The United States, through the First Amendment, is one of those that makes this explicitly clear. It allows you the security to say what you want (even if that is not palatable to the majority) when you like, and to assemble when and where you like. Sometimes this comes back to bite us, as it did in Charlottesville. But most of the time it protects you, the citizen, from bullying by those in power and enables you to speak truth to power when you need to. It affirms your right as a citizen to contribute and to belong to the wider experiment that is American society.

Similarly, the Fourth Amendment—the prohibition against unreasonable search and seizure—allows not only security against bullying and intimidation by the state but also the right to conduct your life as you see fit, absent damage to the security of others. The language of this amendment could not be clearer:

The right of the people to be secure in their persons, houses, papers and effects against unreasonable searches and seizures, shall not be violated.

In the modern era of the Internet, social media, and computing in general, the degree to which this amendment holds is naturally a subject for intense discussion. But in a world where the judiciary upholds the Constitution, more likely than not the prohibition against unreasonable search will persist online and offline—always with the presumption that the actions of one citizen do not unreasonably interfere with the security of another. So, for example, an online stalker that trolls another person with the intent of making them fear for their life cannot necessarily hide behind either this or the First Amendment, given their desire to harm others. But for those nonstalkers among us, even the legions who enjoy online pornography, that is none of the government's business—unless it hurts others (for example, children). The cadence here is clear and simple: You are free to be as you are, do as you want, say what you want—as long as it does not harm others. That is the intent of the Constitution and is the intent of Democratic Libertarianism.

Other amendments to the Constitution, as they accommodated the needs and demands of modern society, mainly kept to this principle. The Thirteenth Amendment abolished slavery. The Fifteenth broadened voting rights. The Nineteenth enabled women's suffrage. Each of these contributed massively to the feeling of belonging in society as a whole. Imagine yourself as a woman in the early twentieth century suddenly having the right to vote. Before the amendment, you were a second-class citizen, subject to the political whims and power of men. Now you are an equal citizen with your own voice—you belong.

But this feeling can easily be destroyed. It's not enough to be enshrined into law; the law has to be enforced and protected. All too often in our history, we have seen rights that should have been protected under law trashed through nonenforcement or, even worse, practices designed to subvert the law. Of these, Jim Crow was the most egregious and appalling. In the era after the Civil War, an era defined by the Thirteenth Amendment and the defeat of the South, the idea was that there would be a period of Reconstruction, overseen by the federal government, in which, among many other things, African-Americans would assume their position as voting and contributing members of society. Despite the appalling record of neglect in this respect by the government of Andrew Johnson, there was a brief period in which African-Americans prospered, building businesses and getting elected to governmental office. In Durham, North Carolina, for example, Parrish Street is known as the Black Wall Street, given the number of African-American financial institutions that were founded there just after the Civil War. Some of these still survive to this day. In the same state, the city of Wilmington elected its first African-American local government.

However, the coup against this democratically elected local government, together with many other atrocities leveled against African-American communities under Jim Crow—lynchings, denial of the vote, public segregation, and humiliation—served to deny this significant population of the nation and the South its constitutional rights for almost another century. Worse, it made this entire population feel as if it did not belong and had no right to belong. Even though the civil rights movement of the 1960s succeeded in getting a white government to pass even more legislation in 1965 (the Civil Rights Act), this feeling persists in much of America today.

When Trayvon Martin was shot by a local vigilante in 2012, many people were outraged—not by the shooting itself but by the fact that the country's first African-American president could say of the event, "If I had a son, he'd look like Trayvon." How dare the president empathize with the black innocent victim of a self-appointed vigilante? When you study that outrage, you realize that when a certain part of society becomes ostracized (or "othered"), society starts to devolve into tribes.

Tribalism takes belonging to an entirely different level. To belong to a tribe is to ascribe "unbelonging" to all those outside of the tribe, and that can easily be leveraged into both hate and violence. You only have to listen to the chants of the white supremacists at Charlottesville to understand how tightly "belonging" is defined in their group and how that gives them permission to hate and "otherize" myriad other groups. Perhaps the most chilling chant they used was "Jews will not replace us!" In parroting a Nazi chant, these sadly indoctrinated people fall into exactly the same trap as those in the Hitler Youth eighty years ago. Their destruction of wider, communal belonging in favor of belonging as a ritual sows insecurity and fear on a national level. And this, of course, is what an extreme Authoritarian Right government wants. It is a play straight out of *The Dictator's Handbook*. By paying off the psychological needs of the tribes (even though you are doing nothing for their actual needs or well-being), you keep a loyal base that is motivated to attack those who they perceive as "others." That increases insecurity in society as a whole, leading to a crumbling of the most fundamental need of all—the feeling of safety. When you feel unsafe, you gravitate to the strongman, the one who promises you that he alone has the ability and the power to solve society's problems. The more you gravitate to him, the more he will give rein to those—consciously or subconsciously—in his tribes to create further chaos. Why is it, do you think, that President Trump resorts so often to the campaign rally, even though he is now president (supposedly) of all the people? It's because he can keep them stoked up, convinced that they are the chosen tribe, ready to cast out the nonbelievers (media included).

How does a Democratic Libertarian society avoid falling into such traps? By casting the feeling of belonging as wide as possible. The Obama administration did this (albeit reluctantly at first) when it put its weight behind same-sex marriage. For far too long, to be LGBTQ in this country—and in others—meant you did not belong. Until all too recently it meant you could not belong in your own family. For too many, that meant living a life of secrecy and of uncertainty. It was only as society's views as a whole began to change that being LGBTQ started to become normal. And it was only then that the government could find the strength to declare itself to be in the same camp and ultimately give the same rights to this community as to everyone else.

The same type of movement gave women the vote and ended government-sanctioned (if not actual) segregation in schools. It is possible we are seeing the beginnings of a similar movement among the young to regulate and control guns. In order to avoid crumbling into a variety of hate-based groups and sects, society has to reconstitute itself from the ground up, facing down major threats to the common good. In a Democratic Libertarian society, government will be there alongside those who are doing the rebuilding. It will cast belonging in the widest possible sense such that no group, no individual, ever has to feel they don't belong. In doing so, it will uphold the Constitution as interpreted across time and through multiple amendments.

The Role of the Judiciary

The concept of a government consisting of three equal branches was one of the Founding Fathers' most significant and enduring principles. The idea that each branch would act as a counterbalance to the others, preventing the dominance of any one of the three, was inspired. But the concept that one of these branches should be the judiciary was perhaps the most inspired of all. It is all too easy for either the executive branch or the legislature on either a federal or state level to be influenced by inducements of money, power, or privilege. Less so the judiciary—but only up to a certain point. And that point is constantly being tested.

The concept of an independent judiciary depends heavily on it being above politics and incorruptible. Judges—especially on courts of appeal and supreme courts—generally have to meet certain standards in terms of qualification. They have to be qualified jurists with a deep and broad track record in administering justice according to the law as it is written and generally interpreted. They have to meet certain standards in terms of probity in their actions on the bench (i.e., they don't take bribes, they don't favor one group over another, and they don't use their position to enrich themselves).

Of course, judges are human beings and they don't always measure up to these standards, but for the most part the judiciary of this country functions as it should. For the most part. There have been some appalling instances over the centuries of courts not measuring up to the Constitution (such as Dredd Scott), and courts have always been a product of the times that produced them. But, as imperfect as the system is, it has generally, if slowly, worked in the direction of justice. But what does "justice" mean here? At its highest level, it means that the courts can act against a slide into tribalism through ensuring equal justice for all, uphold the basic tenets of security under the law, and protect rights given under the Constitution. And those rights are essentially Democratic Libertarian rights—they establish where government can and cannot intervene, and they protect and serve the citizenry.

This concept has its limits. First of all, it means the judiciary has to be above politics. If it is brought into the mainstream of political warfare, thereby opening itself up to the same inducements as those faced by the executive and legislative branches, any idea of the rule of law goes out the window, and with it the constitutional compact between state and citizen of individual security. This is what makes the idea of partisan elections of judges so dangerous—and so deliciously attractive to the Authoritarian Right. A judge who is elected on the basis of his political views and affiliation will undoubtedly be beholden to the party and money interests that seek to place him or her in the position in the first place. Any jurist who has to repay his or her backers (or selectorate) is not one who will uphold the Constitution—period. And that is why those on the Authoritarian Right are so keen to make judicial elections party-based. They want to have control of the judiciary and to make sure that it is under the thumb of the party system rather than doing what it was designed to do, which is to act as an independent third branch of government.

Well, you might say, what about the system for appointing justices to the federal Supreme Court? If anything is political, it is that. The biggest prize a sitting president can get is to appoint one of the nine Supreme Court justices, with Senate approval. And we saw in 2016 just how political that can get, when the Republican Senate refused to consider President Obama's nomination of Merrick Garland for the Supreme Court, preferring to wait months for the presidential election, which, against all odds, the Republicans won. Now, President Trump has had, in his short time in office so far, the great prize of nominating not one but two Supreme Court justices, which commentators see as tilting the Court to the Right for the next three decades.

As the old movie title goes, however, "a funny thing happened on the way to the forum." Very often, Supreme Court justices do not follow the script laid out for them by the party or president that nominated them. Two of the most famous recent examples of this are Sandra Day O'Connor and Anthony Kennedy, both of whom were nominated by President Reagan. While both were expected to hew to the Right, they actually became the most important swing votes on the court in a slew of important cases. The reason? Tenure. Once appointed, a justice (whether it is on the US Supreme Court, a state supreme court, or a court of appeals) is free from political pressure and can apply the law as they see fit according to both the Constitution and their own moral compass. It's not a perfect system, but it works, and it removes the judiciary from the dirt of day-to-day politics. But if, at any stage or at any level of the judicial system, the political-party system intervenes to control this setup, then the foundations of the Constitution become fatally undermined. It is for this reason that, in a Democratic Libertarian society, the independence of the judiciary would be guaranteed and strengthened by means of a constitutional amendment.

The Role of Money

The more money is involved in politics, the more *The Dictator's Handbook* comes into play. Politicians are bound to the money interests that helped elect them and will be expected to pass legislation that favors their donors. The more this happens, the more the system fractures, the less equality of security under the law is protected, the less secure everybody becomes, and the more that tribalism flourishes. In short order, money makes belonging that much more difficult and the purview of the rich rather than the citizenry at large.

In recent years, possibly the worst decision made by the Supreme Court (proving that the system is by no means perfect) was Citizens United. In this 2010 ruling, the court found that the First Amendment prohibits the government from restricting political communications and expenditures by corporations (whether for-profit or nonprofit), labor unions, and other associations. Essentially, the ruling allowed a flood of money to enter into the political system that was not there before. President Jimmy Carter called this the "most stupid" and "most dangerous" decision the Supreme Court had ever made. Why would Carter be so exercised at this development? Because, at base, the type of politics that emerged as a result of the decision go to undermine general belonging and exacerbate belonging in its more destructive tribal sense.

This is due to the fact that money (or an excess of money) in the political system acts in two ways, neither of which are healthy for civil discourse, the exchange of political views, or people's sense of security. The first of these is to open the floodgates of media and advertising expenditure during election season. You might ask, "What is wrong with that?" After all, isn't this one way to inform the electorate and to encourage them to learn about all the issues being debated as a natural course of electing our representatives? The answer to which is yes, but only if the process is on a level playing field and is transparent.

Post–Citizens United, the playing field is most definitely not even. If a corporation or a trade union is to be considered a "person" just as you and I are "persons" under the law, then that assumes an equality of expression and the ability to express and influence views. But you and I are legally limited in terms of the amounts we can contribute to the process, while the same is not true of corporations or unions. Individuals are limited to $2,800 per campaign or candidate in any separate federal election (primaries and general elections being considered "separate"), $5,000 per year to political action committees (PACs), and other limitations where party donations are concerned.[64] While contributions from corporations, unions, and the like are subject to the same limits where donations to a specific candidate are concerned, there are no such limits in how much they can spend in support of so-called super PACs. Legally, these are called "independent expenditure-only committees." There is no cap on how

---

64   Federal Election Commission, February 2019.

much they can raise nor on how much they can spend (even if advertising for or against specific candidates) *as long as they don't coordinate that spending with the campaign itself.* They have to declare who their donors are but, as we shall see, usually find creative ways around this.

What is staggering about these super PACs is the increase in money raised and spent by them over the last decade and a half. The Center for Responsive Politics estimates that between 2002 and 2018, such expenditures rose from just under $17 million to over $1 billion.

But that is not the whole story. What is truly jaw-dropping here is the tiny number of people behind these donations and expenditures. In 2018, there were 2,395 registered super PACs. In terms both of numbers and dollars, they favored the Republicans and the Democrats almost evenly. The top one hundred donors to these organizations raised over 70 percent of their income—and the top 1 percent contributed 95 percent.[65] Who are these people? Some are well known, such as Michael Bloomberg ($90 million) and Jeff Bezos ($10 million). But most are people and organizations that the man or woman on the street would not recognize, such as Sheldon Adelson ($122 million), Thomas Steyer ($70 million), or Richard Uihlein ($38 million), the founder of Uline. In the 2016 election, the total amount spent by the candidates, their parties, and outside groups such as super PACs came to $6.5 billion. Of that, $1.7 billion was spent by outside groups—that is *over a quarter of all money spent.* By any measure, that is a very sizable attempt to wield influence by a very small number of people. The rest of us pale by comparison.

But that's still not the whole story. Unofficial classification of monies donated in election campaigns specifies three broad groups: hard money (the donations that you and I and hundreds of thousands of others give to candidates and their parties); soft money (the type of money that we have just been discussing); and "dark money," a part of soft money whose donors remain obscure and sometimes just plain unknown to the rest of us. Some of

---

65   Center for Responsive Politics, 2019.

this is to be found in the super PACs when the donor is a company or entity (often a limited liability company) whose owners are shrouded by other "shell" organizations. But much of it is also to be found in so-called "social welfare" charities, known by the IRS as 501(c)(4) organizations. These are entities supposedly set up to further a particular social cause who can claim and retain their tax-exempt status as long as "the majority" of their activities do not involve direct political advocacy. This is taken to mean that political advocacy can account for up to 49.9 percent of their activities, although the definition is not well clarified by the law and many creative ways are found around it. These organizations do not have to disclose their donors, even if some of the entities themselves are well known—the NRA being a good example. Others may be obscure charities of which we have never heard and whose donors and backers remain anonymous. In 2016, 501(c)(4) charities injected $165 million into the election cycle.

Since Citizens United, then, a very large proportion of the money being spent to persuade us to vote one way or the other has come from a very small number of people, some of whom are completely unknown to us. This results in an unlevel playing field in two ways:

- A few hundred people and organizations exert an influence that is completely out of proportion with their numbers, arguably drowning out the voices of ordinary citizens. (They also drown us out with interminable attack ads on TV and elsewhere that usually dispense falsehoods by the boatload—sometimes literally, in the case of the "Swift Boat" ads maligning John Kerry in 2004.)

- Voices that dissent from those of the two mainstream parties—voices such as Libertarians or Greens, for example—are barely heard and suffer from a major financial and media deficit in connecting with the electorate.

Such a loaded money-based electoral system is bad enough if the playing field is uneven (particularly if combined with rampant gerrymandering). But there is an even more pernicious effect at work here: the corruption that it introduces into the political system through buying politicians' loyalty to factionalist policies. Once again, *The Dictator's Handbook* comes into play: Who do you keep happy once elected? Your winning coalition. One of the best examples of this in modern-day American politics is the NRA. Despite the fact that a majority of the population (and the NRA's own members) would like to see regulation of gun ownership, the role of the NRA in bank-rolling many (mostly Republican) politicians means that, even in the face of multiple mass shootings, some of which murder kids while at school, those same politicians point-blank refuse to take action to enact such regulations. Why? Because they have taken NRA money and their voting record on the issue of guns has become a Rorschach test of their supposed conservatism. The fact that the NRA is little more than an advocacy body for the gun industry (not gun owners) fazes them not one whit. Most people in this country would say that, while gun ownership is protected under the Second Amendment, there need to be rules and regulations in order to protect the safety and security of all. *The Dictator's Handbook* says who pays, wins. To hell with safety and security.

How then would a Democratic Libertarian society differ where money in politics is concerned? Simply by removing it entirely from the equation. This is not a pie-in-the-sky idea but one which is achieved in a number of countries in a variety of ways. According to IDEA, there are basically three systems other than the American one whereby the influence of money in politics is at least mitigated, if not banished altogether:[66]

1. The "no limits" nations—in these countries (such as Australia, Denmark, and Switzerland) there are no limits either on contributions or spending.

---

66 International Institute for Democracy and Electoral Assistance. Thanks also to *The American Prospect*, April 2014.

However, in most there is also substantial public (i.e., government) funding for the electoral process combined with very strictly limited campaign periods. As such, private money matters much less, and there is limited scope to spend it.

2. "All limits" nations—where there are strict limits both on donations and spending. Examples include Belgium, Canada, and Japan.

3. Limits on spending but not donations—the UK and New Zealand are examples here. You can give as much as you like, but spending is strictly limited. This enables parties to shore up their balance sheets but prevents candidates from becoming dependent on their donors.

In each system there is a built-in barrier against sheer weight of money swaying either an election as a whole or a candidate's dependence on, or loyalty to, a particular donor. Each has its merits and demerits. If I were to choose between the three, I would probably opt for the third option, as it allows for the parties to be healthy (which in turn is healthy for political discourse) but limits candidate dependency. For good measure, I would probably throw in (as the UK does) a strict and short time limit for campaigning. The American system is essentially one continuous election, which means that fund-raising is front and center at pretty much all times.

There is, however, one possible alternative to all of these. Elections at all levels could be funded by the taxpayer. I would hazard a guess that we don't really need to spend $6.5 billion to get the message across in national elections—probably half that would suffice. This would be a trivial expense in the context of a budget measured in the trillions. It would work something like this:

1. In presidential primaries, each candidate for each party's nomination, regardless of size of party, would receive a flat sum for expenditure on administration, campaign management, infrastructure, travel, advertising, and social media.

2. The same would apply to the general election, regardless of how many candidates are standing. This would also level the playing field for smaller parties and independent candidates.

3. A similar structure would be deployed for elections at all other levels.

4. Candidates would have the freedom to decide how to deploy their funds. Surpluses would be returned to their party for general expenses.

5. Parties would be free to raise money for their own general expenses, but these could not be put against individual candidates' campaigns.

6. Campaigning would be limited to one month for local elections, two months for statewide and congressional ones, and six months for presidential ones. Each of these would apply for primaries and the final elections themselves.

This type of structure would allow for a level playing field between parties of all sizes, remove the temptation to be beholden to any one donor, and reduce the time spent on campaigning. It would relieve office holders of the burden of always having to look to the next election and the coffers needed to fight it and allow them to concentrate more on the business at hand—governing.

While this sounds rather regulatory and not so libertarian, the opposite is true. All candidates are treated equally; it opens up the field for minority-party candidates; and it reduces the iniquity of one voice drowning out the others. It also broadens the opportunity to be elected, to get alternative ideas into the discourse, and to be heard. Most important, it eliminates the influence of money on policy making, allowing more politicians to vote according to their conscience, not their wallet. And it will remove much of the burden on voters of having to suffer from an overabundance of election advertising!

Even more important, such an approach would loosen the bonds of tribalism in politics and add to the diversity of political institutions and actors, bringing people into a series of more fluid coalitions. As such, it would broaden the feeling among ordinary voters that their voices count and, as such, broaden the feeling of "belonging."

The Role of Social Media

The last decade has seen the explosion of a phenomenon none of us could have foreseen—the ability around the entire globe of people to connect and share information, feelings, events, thoughts, and outlooks in real time with thousands of other people. Initially seen as a boon to modern life, it is now clear that it can also be a scourge—and it is not clear as to how we can eliminate the one without damaging the other. But one thing is clear: Social media (superficially at least) can boost the feeling of belonging, whether for good or for bad. For millions of people, having a Facebook or Instagram account means keeping up with family, reengaging with old friends, and making new ones. For businesspeople and entrepreneurs, LinkedIn is a boon, allowing them to connect with potential customers and suppliers while also keeping up with the latest trends. Artists and craftspeople now have a market to spread awareness of their capabilities and sell their goods on Etsy. We have also witnessed how powerful social media can be in promoting great social causes such as the Arab Spring. All of this is for the good because it increases our sense of belonging—whether to our families, our circle of friends, or a group of like-minded people seeking to improve lives.

But, as physics teaches us, for each action there is a reaction. For each force, a counterforce. Groups intent on evil can equally as well create a sense of belonging on social media, whether they be white supremacists or jihadists. Unscrupulous politicians can use Twitter to reinforce the prejudices of their base followers or to spread disinformation. And, recognizing its power for good and for casting light on their own particular brands of evil, governments such as those in North Korea, China, and Russia can either shut it down or hunt their enemies through it. Worse, they can seek to destabilize other countries, as the Russians did with US elections in 2016 and as they continue to do elsewhere. Or sects such as ISIS can use it to recruit gullible, seemingly disenfranchised people to commit unbelievable atrocities. Just as social media promotes the well-being of belonging, it can also use it to foster belonging as an evil.

Social media, therefore, is a schizophrenic animal, built for good but also capable of great destruction. And it does both through promoting feelings of belonging. Much of this is its own fault. Facebook, for example, has gone to great lengths to build algorithms that ensure you see only posts that agree with your own outlook, based on your previous posts. As such, you start to exist in an online bubble environment or echo chamber where all you hear are views that accord with your own feelings or prejudices. You don't hear the other side. There is less discourse, not more. We all settle into our own comfortable little tribes and feel that we "belong." Ultimately this is highly corrosive for society. We cease to hear each other, we don't discuss, and we become rabidly polarized to the point that, at family gatherings, we avoid certain subjects like the plague. Thanksgiving and Christmas become holidays that we dread. How on earth is society to deal with this?

A libertarian would tell you that it is what it is. Social media should be allowed to run its course without interference. But democrats (with a small *d*) would say that it contributes to insecurity and division in society that threatens the foundations of the way in which we live and coexist and therefore should be regulated for the greater good.

To be fair, this is not a new phenomenon. The "traditional" media has exhibited many of the same traits from the founding of the republic to this day. There is the responsible media (let's take NPR and PBS as examples, although I am sure many on the Right would disagree with me!) that try to see and project things from a nonbiased point of view. Then there is what I call the "beholden" media (Fox News and, some would say, CNN) that are fixated on pushing a particular vision of political and social life. There is the salacious media, bent on promoting scandal whether true or not, and outright deceptive media (for example, the *National Enquirer*) that seem to peddle lies for the hell of it. This last is a peculiarly American phenomenon, as in most other Western countries it would have been closed down long ago by libel suits. Nonetheless, these are just the modern manifestations of an American media scene that has existed for centuries, where truth battles prejudice, lies, and maliciousness. It has been allowed to exist as such by the First Amendment and, many would argue, has not caused that much damage to the body politic. Why, therefore, treat social media any differently?

Perhaps the problem here is that social media is by its very nature immediate and viral. It can cause enormous damage very quickly and seems incapable of control. And it is very vulnerable to manipulation—more so than traditional media. Witness Russia's attempts at disrupting the electoral process here in the United States, or the Facebook–Cambridge Analytica scandal. In the latter, the data analytics firm Cambridge Analytica sought and obtained permission from Facebook to put a seemingly innocuous quiz on the platform. Some 250,000 people took the quiz and, unbeknownst to them, shared the details of their Facebook friends and their friends and their friends (you get the picture) with the company. In all, Cambridge Analytica harvested the personal details of *eighty million* people, whom it then targeted with tailored political messages during the 2016 campaign. We were not the only country to feel the pernicious tentacles of Cambridge Analytica—nations as far afield as Sri Lanka were also targeted. There are many words to describe their actions (especially when one is, as I am, from the analytics world)—deceptive, destructive, evil. But, ultimately, where does the blame lie, and how can we protect against this happening again?

There is an argument that the fault lies solely with Cambridge Analytica; after all, they manipulated the system to their own advantage. But does fault lie with social media itself, in this case, Facebook? There is an argument that Facebook, Twitter, Instagram, and others should be classified as media channels, just as the *New York Times* and Fox News would be. There should be some standard to which they should be held. Under this scenario, the responsibility should be placed on the channel itself for moderating discussion, setting rules, and strictly curating the data they hold so that it can do no harm. Foster a sense of belonging, yes, but not one that increases insecurity on a widespread basis. Use the power you have to widen that sense of belonging rather than compartmentalize it. And if that means you are classified as a media channel, with all the First Amendment protections that allows you, it also means you have to abide by the rules that govern media as a whole.

Belonging as a Good

Belonging is a fundamental part of being secure as a human being. As such, it is also a fundamental right for an individual in an enlightened society. At its most basic, it is the freedom to be part of something bigger than yourself, where you feel secure. And your personal security—and feeling of security—is government's most sacred duty.

But we ought also to recognize that belonging, if used for the wrong purposes, can be dangerous and corrosive to society. I may get the same feeling of security if I belong to a white supremacist group as I would belonging to a Methodist church, but the reasoning and the outcome would be very different where society is concerned. This is why it is the duty of government to broaden as much as possible the sense of belonging to something much, much bigger—society itself. This is why attempts to suppress voting are anathema to a healthy society. All should be encouraged to vote and to feel as if they belong to the political, social, and national fabric. This is why immigrants should be welcomed into wider society. Why LGBTQ should have the same rights as everyone else. Why race and gender should not matter and should be treated equally.

In the end, we all want to belong, and we should be encouraged by our society and government to do so.

The Belonging pH Scale

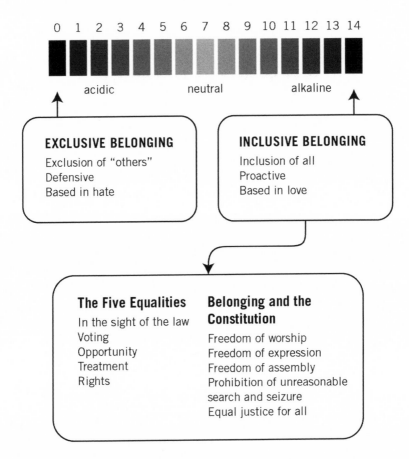

PART FOUR

Self-Esteem and Self-Actualization

(The True American Dream)

17

From Belonging to Esteem

The phrase "to be held in esteem" carries with it rich and profound emotions. It is both the reality and the feeling of other people looking up to you for your achievements, your standing in society, and your role as a model to be emulated by others. It is recognition earned for who you are, what you have achieved, and what you have given. Esteem is a state of being where you are held up as an example to society, usually for your contribution to the greater good. As many have learned, it is something hard won and easily lost.

Usually (but not always) esteem follows belonging. Esteem is derived from extraordinary achievement or contribution in a group in which you feel at home, comfortable, and cherished. But that does not always mean that the group to which you belong is itself generally esteemed. Martin Luther King, for example, first gained esteem among his fellow African-Americans—but they were not a group esteemed at the time. It would take many years (and his death) before he would be more generally esteemed. The same applies to many artists and musicians who may be esteemed among a very small group to which they belong before later becoming highly esteemed in wider society. Think of van Gogh or Mozart—both were esteemed in the small groups in which they lived and worked but only achieved the esteem in which they are now held many years later.

Many people, especially in the United States, mistake esteem for success. Many of those who are indeed successful—but are perhaps loners rather than members of a specific group—believe that they are esteemed. Donald Trump is one of these. A highly successful (we are led to believe) real estate magnate, but very much a lone wolf, he has never achieved the esteem that he feels he deserves. The USSR was, for a time, outwardly successful, becoming a powerful nuclear nation and ruling over a modern-day empire. But it was never accepted as really belonging in the wider group of nations and never achieved the esteem that it too believed was its to have by right. Put simply, material success does not necessarily earn esteem. The key word here is "earn." You earn your right to be looked up to. You do not get it by simply becoming rich or powerful.

Indeed, when asked about who in history they esteem the most, the majority of people do not mention the hugely successful. Instead, they cite those who they perceive have given of themselves for the betterment of society and the world: Ghandi, for his courage and example in leading nonviolent protest against British rule of India; Churchill, for his leadership in the Second World War; Mother Theresa, for her devotion to the poor of India; Nobel Prize winners, for their contribution to learning, science, and peace.

But how does this relate to "*self*-esteem"? True self-esteem—the penultimate level in Maslow's hierarchy—is a feeling of receiving recognition for one's achievements and contributions. It is the recognition that others hold you in esteem and that perhaps you have done something to earn that status. It is a feeling that you have maybe made a difference. Note that the key issue here is what others think of you and what you may have done to earn their approval. It is not what you think of yourself absent any external evidence or societal respect. Just because you believe you are a successful mogul does not equate to self-esteem in a vacuum. Rather, that is called arrogance and self-aggrandizement. Real self-esteem is humble, yet not blind to the fact that you have indeed made a contribution. But, to have made that contribution, you have to realize you are indeed part of a group (however small), and that group played a part in your achievements by making you feel you belonged.

For self-esteem to even be a possibility, a number of conditions must exist that enable individuals and entities to achieve things that first earn them the esteem of others. These can be personal, institutional, national, or even global. The coming together of these conditions (in any number of combinations) leads to a state where the individual concerned can feel fulfilled and, in doing so, earn the right to self-esteem.

In a *personal* setting, the individual needs the freedom and/or the opportunity to achieve things that are above and beyond the ordinary. *Institutions* usually function best in an atmosphere of freedom to experiment and to act, spurred on by and uplifting the individuals that make them up. Note that there are caveats in both the sentences above—"and/or" and "usually." This is because human beings are capable of the most extraordinary acts and achievements even in the face of the greatest hardships and repression. On an individual level, think of Nelson Mandela, who braved over a quarter of a century on a barren island in inhumane conditions only to then lead his country in the most amazing bloodless revolution. Or think, on an institutional level, of Doctors Without Borders, whose personnel brave extreme danger every day bringing health care to war-torn and disease-ravaged parts of the world without thought for their own safety. These are people who act on an extraordinary level, going above and beyond to give to others. They do not act in safety or security, but rather in its absence.

An interesting twist to this, however, is that behind each of these people and institutions are usually others—however distant they may be—who are providing material and/or emotional support of the type that, in the end, makes them feel they still belong to something bigger than themselves. In the case of Doctors Without Borders, it is their loyal backers who supply them with money and material support month after month. In Mandela's case, it was the support of the international community, organizing boycotts of South African goods and not letting up on noisy protests all around the world. Even in the most desperate cases, such as those of Aleksandr Solzhenitsyn when he was in the gulags or Dietrich Bonhoeffer, the Protestant theologian who denounced the Nazis and paid with his life, there were groups (however small and powerless) who supported them and made them feel that they belonged. They all were esteemed, some more so after death than before; they all earned their esteem; they all had a right to feel fulfilled and therefore to have some measure of self-esteem.

In more normal times and situations than those encountered by Mandela, Doctors Without Borders, Solzhenitsyn, or Bonhoeffer, it is the freedom allowed by society itself that allows for such achievement and for the right to self-esteem to be earned. It is the security afforded by that freedom that sets the conditions in which both individuals and institutions can reach the heights of achievement that set them apart. Most people who achieve high esteem (and whatever self-esteem they derive from that) are not working within the confines of a dictatorship or in war zones. Rather, they are pushing the boundaries of science or music or technology, secure in their ability to do so and supported by the groups to which they belong, be they universities, companies, or society at large. It is therefore no surprise that the top five nations of size (excluding the likes of Luxembourg and the Faroe Islands) in terms of most Nobel Prizes per capita are Switzerland, Sweden, Denmark, Norway, and Austria. Among the large nations, the country with the most Nobels per head is the United Kingdom. All of these are countries that stress freedom and security, most especially in terms of their social and economic frameworks. They are also for the most part countries where national pride revolves around achievements that better humanity, where public ethics are important, and where the standing of the nation as a whole in the eyes of the world is important—that is, countries that themselves have a certain amount of self-esteem for what they contribute, not what they own. (Where the UK is concerned, I am obviously talking about the nation as it is today, not as it was in its imperial times. The same goes for Austria.)

Esteem and self-esteem exist alongside one another in societies where there is an atmosphere of security, where individuals and organizations are encouraged to push boundaries, and where there is a sense of belonging to a nation and society that appreciates, welcomes, and emulates them. That society is a Democratic Libertarian society where democracy guarantees freedom paired with justice and where libertarianism allows for freedom of movement, thought, and expression.

18

Reaching the Pinnacle: Self-Actualization

America is a nation built on self-actualization. For that matter, so are Britain, France, Italy, and any other number of nations. But what do we mean by "self-actualization"? The emphasis here is on "self," but not self-ish. Self-actualization is when you reach the pinnacle of your abilities, contribution, and humanness. It is when you become the best that you can ever be, and in the wake of that, you leave your mark on humanity. You leave the world a better place for your having been in it. Many Americans have reached that pinnacle, and their legacy has lived on way beyond their physical life span—Thomas Edison for having given us electricity. Martin Luther King for having broken the dam on civil rights. Billy Graham for having brought us to confront our own spirituality. Rosa Parks for having refused to change seats. We could name thousands of others from all around the world—Marie Curie, Nelson Mandela, Beethoven, Shakespeare, Alan Turing. The list goes on and on.

But self-actualization is not solely the province of the famous. It is to be found all around us, in our schoolteachers, professors, scientists, nurses, doctors, firefighters, inventors, designers, and even in our school bus drivers, chefs, public defenders, and janitors. For these are people who reach deep into themselves to bring out the best in others and who, in however small a way, leave a lasting mark. How many of us can name a schoolteacher, for example, who inspired us and who changed the course of our lives? How many can name a boss who, through inspiration and small kindnesses, enabled our careers? Or a parent, grandparent, or relative who taught us a life skill? Self-actualization is what drives society and those within it to reach further and better. Sometimes it is rewarded with fame and riches, but for the most part, it is not. For the most part, it is its own reward.

But for self-actualization to exist, the society in which it can flourish and which it can affect for the better has to be one in which freedom and security are paramount. People need to feel secure in reaching to be their best and in applying their talents for the betterment of others. It is very difficult to be self-actualized in a dictatorship such as Russia, Zimbabwe, or Iran, where the very act of your trying to reach your best might be seen as a threat to the mediocrity that is in power. That is not to say that we don't see self-actualization in these countries. We do. And usually, the people involved are some of the most brave and selfless that you will ever encounter, determined to serve their human brethren even at the cost of their own safety and lives. But these are salmon that swim upstream. Usually, those that unleash betterment on the world as their everlasting legacy are those who achieve self-actualization in free, secure, democratic societies.

To achieve those societies, however, takes dedicated hard work, perseverance, and watchfulness. There has to be physical security, economic security, emotional security, an absence of fear, a promotion of freedom, and a feeling of belonging. Any of these can be challenged—from within or without—at any time, and we have to be prepared to fight back to defend and secure these freedoms at all times. Not to do so is to acquiesce in a slippery slope to totalitarianism, to go along with *The Dictator's Handbook* and to be complicit in our own downfall.

All of us—every single member of a free, secure, and democratic society—are charged with defending that society and securing the conditions in which all of us not only belong but can reach the pinnacle of our talents to the betterment of others.

I was lucky enough in my youth to go to a unique school in the Sussex countryside in England called Christ's Hospital. Established as a benevolent foundation in 1552 by King Edward VI to care for and educate the orphans of London, the school still exists to this day as a place where disadvantaged children can receive an excellent education and learn invaluable life skills for free or at a very low cost. As young adults graduate at the age of seventeen or eighteen, they receive what is known as "The Charge":

I charge you never to forget the great benefits that you have received in this place, and in time to come, according to your means, to do all that you can to enable others to enjoy the same advantage. And remember that you carry with you, wherever you go, the good name of Christ's Hospital.

This is a clarion call to self-actualization—to reach for your best and then to deploy that to the benefit of others. Whoever we are, we receive blessings and benefits along the way, and it is ultimately our duty to pass the legacy of those along to those who travel with us or who follow us. To be able to do so, we need the kind of society that encourages that to happen, secure in the freedom we enjoy and the sense of belonging that we feel. That is the sacred "charge" of a Democratic Libertarian society, and that is the charge to which America can and should aspire.

Esteem, Self-Esteem, and Self-Actualization

We are all responsible for protecting, promoting, and ensuring the security of society as a whole in order to let the genie of self-actualization out of the bottle.

BELONGING

ESTEEM
(Earned, Hard Won, Easily Lost)

FREEDOM, OPPORTUNITY
& SECURITY

SELF-ESTEEM

SELF-ACTUALIZATION

HARD WORK

PERSERVERANCE

WATCHFULNESS

The Democratic Libertarian Manifesto

The Democratic Libertarian Manifesto for 2020

Our Values and Philosophy

- We recommit to government of the people, by the people, and for the people.

- A Democratic Libertarian government will create the framework for security both for society and the individual—and then get out of the way.

- We will govern to maximize security, esteem, and happiness.

- In doing so, we will resuscitate the Constitution for the twenty-first century.

- We will abstain from ideology.

- We will govern so that everyone has equal rights to security, esteem, and self-actualization. But law-making will be restricted to providing that framework—all other decisions will be left to individuals and/or the smallest governing entity (city, county, school board).

- There will be no federal or state interference in questions that are fundamentally social or religious.

- We will create the widest selectorate and winning coalitions so as to involve the maximum number of people in choosing our governments.
- We are committed to servant leadership (authentic and inspirational, yet humble and honest).
- Our values are rooted in liberty, inclusiveness, empathy, community, supportiveness, respect, listening, patriotism, inspiration, and security.
- Security is a social contract. Everyone has the right to live in a free, secure world in return for payment of taxes and real involvement in community.

Key Goals

- Reversing climate change, as well as promoting strong environmental stewardship and respect for this world and its ecosystems
- Promoting educational excellence in pre-K through grade twelve and in universities but also through remedial retraining for the populations most affected by change
- Providing the best health care system (both preventive and palliative) in the world
- Ensuring the most modern, up-to-date, and safe infrastructure, both physical and digital
- Sensibly regulating financial services to prevent banks from trading on their own account and make them accountable to their depositors and customers
- Balancing the rights and interests of capital and labor, both through incentives and regulation
- Ensuring equity of taxation rates

- Pursuing monetary policy that maintains stability in the markets, especially where interest rates are concerned

- Remembering the second half of Keynes's equation, which was to build surpluses in good times for when they are needed in the bad times (i.e., not to indulge in knee-jerk tax cuts whenever everything seems to be going well)

Physiological Security

The underlying thinking is that protecting the physiological security of all in our society saves us money. Therefore, protecting that security will always be put first—in law and order, the judiciary, housing, health, the environment, and social welfare.

Specific priorities:

- Reassume society's responsibility for mental health care

- Take the mentally ill out of jails and prisons, and reinvest in mental health centers and prevention

- Recommit to environmental protection—reaffirm US participation in the Paris Agreement, strengthen the Environmental Protection Agency, and reverse environmentally damaging laws and executive orders

- Act to mitigate the underlying causes of homelessness and hunger

- Provide affordable housing in every city

- Provide resources for rehousing the homeless

- Facilitate reentry of the homeless into society

- Legislate a living minimum wage

- Legalize and regulate drugs, including surrogates and antidotes, and distribute through state-controlled facilities (and so suck the profits out of the illegal drug trade and deprive syndicates and gangs of their reason for being)

- Revisit drug-related and nonviolent-offense sentencing laws
- Set Big Hairy Audacious Goals to reclaim the security and sustainability of our environment
- Recognize and enshrine the rights of all aspects of our ecosystem—rivers, mountains, lakes and oceans

Physical Security

- Recommit to Pax Americana
- Reduce defense spending but require matched increases by NATO and other partners
- Require law enforcement to serve and protect all without regard to race, gender, class, or status
- Demilitarize the police
- Accept the reality of the Second Amendment but act to regulate gun ownership and use—define what types of guns are acceptable and determine who can own them, how they should be trained, where they can buy them, and where they can carry them
- Abolish the death penalty

Financial Security

- Rebalance the influence of capital and labor
- Simplify the tax system into three simple income bands without deductions

- Ban the use of the tax system for social or other legislation
- Pass a constitutional amendment to mandate the balancing of aggregate budgets over a period of ten years
- Reduce—and eventually end—reliance on sales taxes
- Simplify and segregate the banking system
- Continue and strengthen the FDIC
- Severely prosecute financial crimes and corruption
- Balance regulations to ensure security but at the same time promote competitiveness
- Actively promote innovation, including through government programs

Educational Security

- Move education funding from property taxes to income taxes
- Weight funding toward poorer neighborhoods
- Treat education as an investment in future growth
- Educate the whole child, reduce the use of standardized tests, and judge schools by life outcomes of their students
- Require states to spend a statutory minimum of their budgets on education
- Allow both state and private education, but not cofunding
- Raise teacher pay to reflect their importance in society

Health Security

- Institute a single-payer system—everyone covered for the same things with the private insurance layer removed

- Allow private health system in parallel but not cofunding

- Establish optional long-term-care funds (tax-exempt unless liquidated for non-health use)

- Increase funding for Alzheimer's and dementia research

Social Security

- Institute nationwide social security benefits that treat everyone equally in terms of unemployment benefits, retraining, relocation for new jobs, drug rehabilitation

- Remove federal and state governments from moral, social, or religious lawmaking (e.g., abortion) and pass these down to county level

- Reinforce separation of church and state; the state should become religion-neutral, and laws based in religious mores will not be considered (under constitutional amendment if necessary) by federal or state legislatures

Reinforcement of Belonging

EQUALITY IN THE SIGHT OF THE LAW

- Reform laws that treat races or other segments of the population differently—for example, the criminalization of drugs

- Pursue comprehensive immigration reform to allow a path to citizenship for illegal immigrants already in the country
- Redesign the legal immigration system to retain more of those from other countries that we educate and train
- Strengthen overstay immigrant tracking
- Invest heavily in countries from which most immigrants come to reduce their need to emigrate
- Set clear humanitarian and asylum rules for acceptance of refugees

EQUALITY IN VOTING

- Institute a federal system to independently draw electoral maps to standard rules
- Institute federal rules on voting protocols and processes (e.g., early voting, mail ballots, number of voting days)
- Punish voter intimidation by law
- Abolish the electoral college

EQUALITY OF OPPORTUNITY

- Provide equal access to quality, funded education and health care

EQUALITY OF TREATMENT

- Do not deny any section of society the rights available to others—e.g., marriage, legal rights, protection under the law
- Mandate equality of pay regardless of gender, race, or sexual orientation

EQUALITY OF RIGHTS

· Apply constitutional rights equally to all

Judicial Security

· Ban partisan elections for judges on any court
· By constitutional amendment, secure the independence of the judiciary

Electoral Security

· Eliminate private funding of elections
· Repeal Citizens United
· Institute taxpayer funding for all candidates
· Institute time-limited campaigns

Security in the Digital World

· Classify social media as media channels and put them on an equal footing with traditional media

Epilogue

On March 15, 2019, a twenty-eight-year-old Australian self-confessed fascist attacked two mosques with military-style automatic weapons in the New Zealand city of Christchurch. At the end of the attack, which he live-streamed on Facebook, fifty people lay dead and another fifty were wounded. New Zealand, a quintessential and highly successful Democratic Libertarian country, reacted in horror. Such acts of terror were hitherto unheard of in this peace-loving nation.

But what was remarkable was the reaction of the young prime minister, Jacinda Ardern. Eschewing the tendency of most politicians to paint the shooter as an enemy or to declare a "war" on terrorism, she both acted fast to close the loopholes that had allowed this person to act as he did and started to heal the nation through a strong message of belonging. The first came in the form of rapidly enacted laws to ban the types of weapons used in the attack. The second came in a series of extraordinary messages to the nation.

Many of those who will have been directly affected by this shooting may be migrants to New Zealand. They may even be refugees here. They have chosen to make New Zealand their home, and it is their home. They are us.

We cannot know your grief, but we can walk with you at every stage. We can and will surround you with aroha, manaakitanga[67] and all that makes us.

Note that she chose not to "otherize" any sections or types of people but that she used the language of inclusion, of belonging. Note the deliberate use of the word "us."

This is a Democratic Libertarian leader at her best.

---

67   Kindness, compassion, generosity.

Acknowledgments

P ublishing a book is a huge team effort, and there are a lot of unsung heroes behind the scenes who deserve recognition.

I would particularly like to thank the whole team at Greenleaf Publishing for their expertise and support. A friendlier and more professional crew would be difficult to find. So, my profound thanks to Justin Branch, Jen Glynn, Erin Brown, Rachael Brandenburg, Tiffany Barrientos, Olivia McCoy, and O'Licia Parker-Smith. You all were an inspiration.

Similarly, to all the highly creative people at Smith Publicity, many thanks for taking on an author unknown in the field of American politics, having faith, and working so brilliantly to shine a light on this book. Thanks to Dan Smith, Mike Onorato, and their entire team.

In addition to the professionals that guide you, there are also those who either equipped you to be able to write on a particular topic or who provided you with support, constructive criticism, and guidance. In the first camp are all the professors and tutors at Oxford, who not only taught me about politics and economics but also taught me how to think. To them I am hugely indebted, especially to Dr. Janet Morgan, herself a highly acclaimed author, and (posthumously) Lord Norman Crowther-Hunt and Dr. Walter Eltis. In the second camp are the people who along the way have graciously read the manuscript, made suggestions, and, at times, challenged me on both facts and opinions. I am particularly indebted to Michael Thompson, Kumar Mehta, Will Leach, Reg Baker, Kathi Love, and Gabi Coatsworth for their time, dedication, and advice.

Above all, I could not have even contemplated this venture without the total support, patience, and love of my wife, Johnnie. She doggedly read each chapter as it emerged, challenged me, and boosted me during the low times. She is my inspiration.

About the Author

Growing up in South Africa as the son of a prominent anti-apartheid activist, Simon Chadwick has firsthand experience of living in a totalitarian society. After residing and working in the United States for twenty-eight years, he increasingly noticed distinct and unnerving parallels to his early upbringing in the way US politics was developing. Upon the election of Donald Trump, he decided he could no longer sit on the fence; he became a citizen and started to write this book.

A corporate CEO, management consultant, and editor-in-chief of a global magazine, Chadwick gained his MA in philosophy, politics, and economics from Oxford University. He is married to a Louisianan and lives in North Carolina.